P9-DDH-080

If you have questions or comments about material in this book, I will be glad to answer them. Please call or write:

Doc Fizzix

1500 Laurel Oak Loop
Round Rock, TX 78664

(512) 218-0454

http://www.docfizzix.com

Alden J. Balmer is Doc Fizzix

Seventh Edition (2008 edition)

Copyright © 2002 Alden J. Balmer and Mike Harnisch

All rights reserved. No part of this publication may be reproduced, stored in retrieval systems, or transmitted, in any form or by any means, electronic, mechanical, photocopying, recording, or otherwise, without the prior written permission of the publisher.

ISBN 0-9656674-2-1

Printed by
Armstrong Printing
Austin, Texas

by Al Balmer

Drawings by Mike Harnisch

Doc Fizzix Publishing Company

Round Rock, Texas

Table of Contents

Table of Contents

Table of Contents

Table of Contents

SAFE USE OF HAND TOOLS

Hand tools are easy and safe to use when they are used properly. Please inform yourself about safe use of hand tools by reading ahead and by consulting your teacher or mentor. Described below are some commonly used hand tools and some dangerous situations that can result if they are not used properly.

Safety Glasses **The most important safety aid is inexpensive and available at any hardware store or from your shop teacher.**

Hot Glue Gun Very useful for quickly fastening different materials together with a reasonably strong bond. Hot glue guns can cause **minor burns** if the gun nozzle or hot glue touches the skin.

Soldering Iron Useful for making electrical connections. Soldering irons can cause **minor burns** if the soldering tip, or hot solder, touches the skin.

Electric Hand Drill Hand drills are useful for placing holes in materials and might be used in the fabrication of wheels, for example. **Wear safety glasses.** If too much force is applied, drill bits can break, launching fragments into the air. Material removed by the drill bit can also become airborne. Students using hand drills should work a safe distance from students who are not wearing safety glasses. **Clamp work securely.** A spinning drill bit can grab the workplace and yank it around if it is not properly clamped in place, resulting in injuries, especially if the workplace has sharp edges. A small vice or clamp is useful for this purpose. **Note what is underneath the piece being drilled.** Be sure that drilling is done into a secure block of scrap wood or into a clear space.

Hacksaw Hacksaws are useful for cutting a variety of materials. **Wear safety glasses.** Removed material could become airborne. **Keep hands away from the cutting zone.** The blade can jump and cause minor hand injuries. **Clamp work securely.** This removes any inclination to hold the workplace near the cutting zone and allows better control of the tool.

Wire Clippers These tools are useful for cutting wire and thin shafts. If both sides of the piece are not securely held, it may shoot out. Orient the tool so that the section being clipped is aimed at the floor or held in some other way.

Utility or "Exacto" Knives Useful for cutting cardboard, foamboard, etc.
Cut away from yourself (i.e., don't draw the blade towards your hand or any other part of your body). **Store tools safely.** Avoid leaving exposed blades on table surfaces. Use a handle with a retractable blade if possible.

Acknowledgments

I dedicate this book to my mother, Dr. Karen Ostlund, who has so unselfishly given her love to me. Without her help I would never be where I am today.

A special thanks goes to Mark Daniels and David Hailes for all their help and ideas in the making of this book. Mark and David teach at McNeil High School in Round Rock, Texas. Mark teaches mathematics and David teaches science. It is their dedication to their subject matters that I envy the most. They are truly the best in their profession.

About the Author

Alden J. Balmer is an award-winning physics teacher at McNeil High School in the Round Rock Independent School District, located in Round Rock Texas. His mouse trap car competitions have helped increase the physics enrollment at McNeil High School from one class of 15 students to 10 classes of 25 students. In 1996, Al Balmer was selected as the most outstanding science teacher in the State of Texas; this was in part because of his creative approach to teaching science and his ability to hook students into science with creative engineering projects such as the mouse trap car competition. Al Balmer and his students have appeared on locally and nationally aired television programs and at national science conventions, discussing how to build and race mouse-trap cars. In this book, Al Balmer (Doc Fizzix) discusses all the important elements that need to be considered in order to construct the perfect mouse trap car. From reading this book you will also learn the basic conceptual concepts that are needed to construct your own mouse trap car and how those concepts relate to mouse trap car engineering. Al Balmer has built over 100 different mouse trap vehicles and extensively tested each car to determine the important variables that needed to be considered in order to achieve maximum performance.

About the Illustrator

Mike Harnisch is a published cartoonist and freelance artist. His cartoons have appeared in the *Austin American-Statesman, The Daily Texan*, and several other national and local publications. He created his cartoon character, "Fred," at the age of 8, and has been drawing ever since. Mike's ultimate dream is to become a syndicated cartoonist, and his hard work and perseverance thus far may help him realize that dream. In 1996, Mike's cartoon, "Wet Feet," helped him earn the National College Media award for Best Cartoon Strip and he continues to draw daily and weekly strips along with illustrations. Mike lives in Austin, Texas and loves the Beatles, the Buffalo Bills, and Erin, his girlfriend.

What is a **Mouse-Trap Car** and **How does it Work?**

A mouse-trap car is a vehicle that is powered by the energy that can be stored in a wound up mouse-trap spring. The most basic design is as follows: a string is attached to a mouse-trap's lever arm and then the string is wound around a drive axle causing the mouse-trap's spring to be under tension. Once the mouse-trap's arm is released, the tension of the mouse-trap's arm pulls the string off the drive axle causing the drive axle and the wheels to rotate, propelling the vehicle. This most basic design can propel a vehicle several meters for any first-time builder. But in order to build vehicles that can travel over **100 meters** or extreme speed cars that can travel **5 meters in less than a second,** you must learn about some of the different variables that affect the performance of a mouse-trap car. For example, how does friction affect the overall distance that a vehicle can travel? How does the length of the mouse-trap's lever arm affect the performance? By reading each section of this book you will learn about many of the different variables that will affect a vehicle's performance. Also you will learn how to modify different variable in order to build a top performing vehicle.

LEVER ARM

STRING

PULLING FORCE

STRING WRAPPED AROUND DRIVE AXLE

MOTION

Getting Started

Why build a mouse-trap car? Building mouse-trap cars allows you to experience the process of design and engineering first-hand. When you build a vehicle, you have to start with an ideas and then turn that idea into a real-life model that works. Building a mouse-trap car is an advanced form of problem solving with two main ingredients:

1. **You don't know what the problems are.** *Many of the problems in building a mouse-trap car will be discovered and solved as you go along; each person's challenges will be different.*

2. **There is never one right answer!**

One last thought before we get started. Throughout the construction of your car, you will have to deal with trade-offs. For example, building a car that accelerates quickly usually means sacrificing fuel efficiency. When applying any of the ideas and hints in this book to the construction of a mouse-trap car, understand that any extreme exaggeration of just one variable may have a large negative effect on the performance of your vehicle. **It is best to find a harmonious balance between each variable through repeated experimentation.** Experimentation is essential in order to achieve maximum performance. Experiment often and early, don't worry about making mistakes! Making a mistake is a learning experience. Keep in mind you will not know many of the problems until you encounter them as you build your car. Engineering is a process by which ideas are tested and retested in an effort to produce the best working product. A good engineer knows one way to get something to work and 99 ways it won't work. **Do not be afraid to try your different ideas; your tested ideas will lead you to success!** Also, by understanding the basic conceptual physics concepts presented in this book, you will be able to make good decisions about building the perfect car. **Don't delay, get started!**

Getting Started

Almost any materials can be used in the construction of a good mouse-trap car. It is up to the designer to determine the appropriate application of such materials. Sizes, lengths, diameters, widths, and kinds of materials are more-or-less left up to the designer. The human imagination is a wonderful gift, and our own ingenuity allows us to take ordinary objects with functions different from what were intended and turn them into components of a working machine. For example, a compact disc is a good device for storing information and playing it back, but it also makes a great wheel. Good luck!

Getting Started

Tools of the Trade

- *Dremel Tool*
- *Hobby Knife*
- *Files*
  - *Round*
  - *Square*
  - *Knife*
- *Power Drill*
- *Drill Bits*
- *Glue*
  - *Super Glue*
  - *Wood Glue*
  - *Hot Glue*
  - *Rubber Cement*
- *Coping Saw or Hack Saw*
- *Pliers*

Motion

Motion occurs all around us yet it is hard to describe and explain. More than 2000 years ago the Greeks try to describe motion but failed because they did not understand the concept of **rate of change**. Today we describe motion as **rates of change** or some quantity divided by time. Speed is the measure of how fast something is traveling or the rate at which distance is being covered, another way of describing speed is to say that it is the distance that is being covered per time where the word **per** means divided by. In most cases, when you calculate the **speed** of a mousetrap racer you get an **average speed** over some distance, you begin timing at some predetermined starting point and then you stop timing at some predetermined ending point. This method does not tell you the **instantaneous speed** of your vehicle along any point of its motion it only tells you the **average speed** over your timing distance. In everyday conversations we tend to use the words speed and **velocity** interchangeably but it needs to be pointed out the speed and velocity are slightly different. Unlike speed velocity tells you direction; example, to say an object is traveling at 55 mi/h is to give the objects speed only, to say an object is traveling at 55 mi/h due north is to give the object velocity. By adding the direction of an object motion we change it from speed to velocity. Why is this small distinction of direction important in the study of motion? If the velocity of an object is changing then there is another way to describe the objects motion and it is called **acceleration**, the rate at which velocity is changing. Velocity is changing when any of the following conditions occurs, there is a **change in speed**, or there is a **change in direction**. A car traveling in a circle at a constant speed has a changing direction so even though its speed is constant its direction is not, so it is accelerating. **Acceleration is something you can feel**, when you step on the gas pedal or break pedal in a car you feel yourself accelerate. Also, when you turn the steering wheel of a car you change your direction and you feel acceleration so we say that accelerations are changes in speed and direction.

Motion

Lab #1 - Chasing the Mouse

Purpose

To analyze the motion of a mousetrap powered vehicle over 5 meters.

Equipment Needed

Ticker Timer
Ticker Tape
Meter Stick
Stopwatch

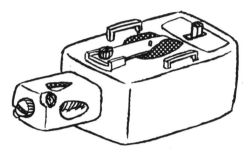

Discussion

In this experiment you will collect data from your mousetrap car using a ticker timer. A ticker timer is a device that makes marks on a ticker tape at equal intervals of time. A long piece of ticker tape will be attached to the back of your mousetrap vehicle. As your vehicle is in motion the ticker timer will leave a series of marks on the tape that is attached to your vehicle. Because the time between each mark is the same, a variety of variables can be measured and calculated from the position of each mark. I recommend analyzing the motion of your car over a five meter distance. After your vehicle has made its run, you will be measuring the distance from the first mark to each of the following marks. Velocity is the rate at which your vehicle is covering distance. The greater the rate, the more distance that is being covered per time. The average velocity is the travel distance divided by the travel time. The actual velocity at each mark is calculated from the average velocity by using Formula #2 from the list of formulas. Acceleration is the rate at which your vehicle is changing velocity. In order to find the acceleration you will have to first find the change in velocity between each point using Formula #3. By dividing the change in velocity for each interval, you will calculate the acceleration between each mark (Formula #4).

Motion

Formulas

Formula #1: $\quad \bar{v} = \dfrac{\Delta d}{\Delta t} \qquad \bar{v} = \dfrac{d_{t_f} - d_{t_0}}{\Delta t}$

Formula #2: $\quad \bar{a} = \dfrac{\Delta v}{\Delta t} \qquad \bar{a} = \dfrac{v_{t_f} - v_{t_0}}{\Delta t}$

Using a Stopwatch: Alternative Approach

6

 I suggest timing the vehicle over 5 meters if you plan on using a ticker timer, but if you have a long-distance car that travels great distances, you should not use the ticker timer because the vehicle will become too heavy by pulling of the long ticker tape. You can collect data with an alternative approach: Mark out the floor with masking tape every meter or two meters, depending on the distance that your car will go.

Using a stopwatch that can handle split times, walk along side your mousetrap car and call out the time at each mark on the floor. A partner should be recording the times as you relay them using the split-time function. Calculations are the same, but realize that in this example the distance was held constant and not the time.

Please take note: It is assumed that the experimenter uses standard S.I. units for all activities.

Motion

The Set-up

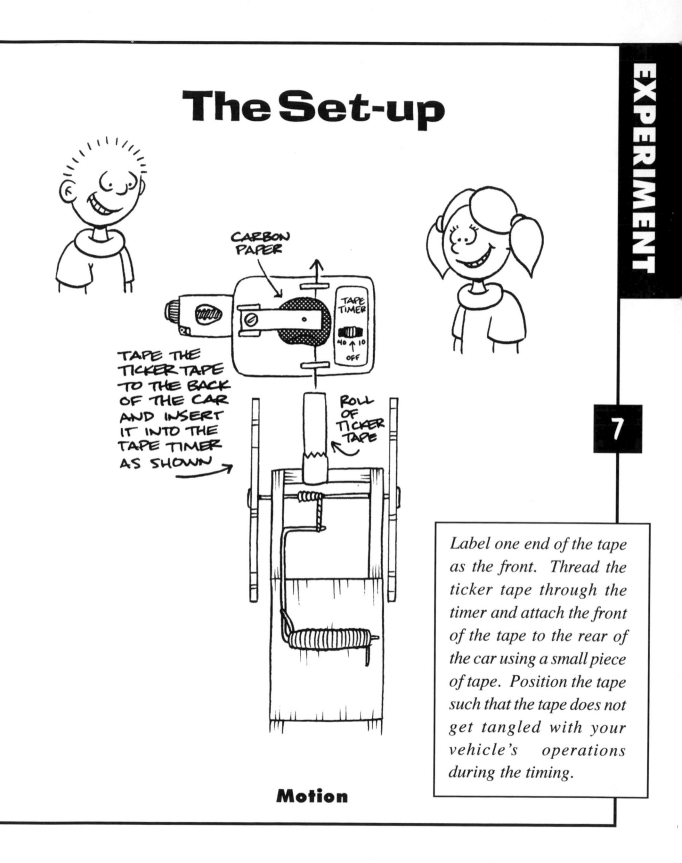

CARBON PAPER

TAPE TIMER

40 ↑ 10
OFF

TAPE THE TICKER TAPE TO THE BACK OF THE CAR AND INSERT IT INTO THE TAPE TIMER AS SHOWN

ROLL OF TICKER TAPE

Label one end of the tape as the front. Thread the ticker tape through the timer and attach the front of the tape to the rear of the car using a small piece of tape. Position the tape such that the tape does not get tangled with your vehicle's operations during the timing.

Motion

Ticking Away the Time

Step 1: Determine the distance for which the data will be collected. Tear off enough ticker tape to cover the distance of the timing.

Step 2: Select or determine the frequency of the ticker timer. The frequency of the ticker tape determines the time between each mark. If the frequency is 10Hz, the time between marks is 0.1s. If the frequency is 60Hz, the time between marks is 1/60 s. Record this frequency in your data table under "time."

Step 3: Label one end of the tape as the front. Thread the ticker tape through the timer and attach the front of the tape to the rear of the car using a small piece of tape. Position the tape such that the tape does not get tangled with your vehicle's operations during the timing.

Step 4: Place your vehicle at the start line. Line up the ticker timer directly behind the vehicle tape. Straighten the ticker tape behind the timer so that is passes through the timer without binding. Turn the ticker timer on and then release the vehicle. Remove the tape from the vehicle after the run.

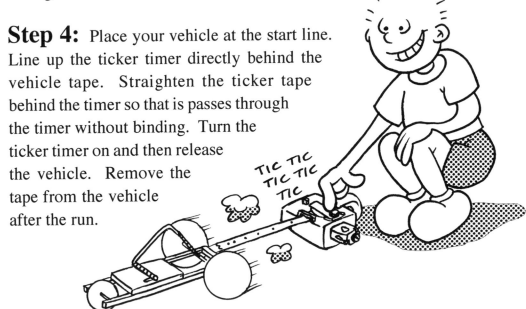

Motion

EACH DOT GETS FURTHER AND FURTHER APART, SHOWING ACCELERATION OF THE CAR, SO a EQUALS CHANGE IN VELOCITY OVER TIME...

... OR $a = \dfrac{\Delta v}{t}$!

Step 5: From the front of the ticker tape, darken each mark and label as follows: $t_0, t_1, t_2, t_3, t_4, t_5, \ldots t_n$.

Step 6: Design a data table where you can record the following: total time (t), distance between marks (Δd), total distance (d), velocity at mark (vf), change in speed from previous mark (Δv), acceleration between marks (a).

Data Table #1

Total Time	Change in Time	Change in Distance	Total Distance	Change in Velocity	Acceleration
$t_1=$	$t_{0,1}=$	$\Delta d_{0,1}=$	$d_1=$	$\Delta v_{f,1}=$	$a_{0,1}=$
$t_2=$	$t_{1,2}=$	$\Delta d_{1,2}=$	$d_2=$	$\Delta v_{f,2}=$	$a_{1,2}=$
$t_3=$	$t_{2,3}=$	$\Delta d_{2,3}=$	$d_3=$	$\Delta v_{f,3}=$	$a_{2,3}=$

Step 7: Measure the distance from the first mark (t_0) to the second mark (t_1) and record this as the distance between marks ($\Delta d_{0,1}$). Measure the distance from the points (t_1) and the (t_2) and record this as (t_2) distance between marks ($\Delta d_{1,2}$). Measure the distance between each of the following marks and record as the distance between marks ($\Delta d_{2,3}, \Delta d_{3,4}, \Delta d_{4,5} \ldots \Delta d_n$).

Step 8: Add the change in distance between $d_{0,1}$ and record as d_1 total distance. Add the change in distance between $d_{0,1}$ and $d_{1,2}$ and

Recommendations
*Try to set-up a **spread sheet** on a computer in order to handle your data more **efficiently**.*

Motion

$d_{1,2}$ and record as d_2 total distance. Add the total distance between $d_{1,2}$ and $d_{2,3}$ and record as d_3 total distance. Continue this approach until you have the total distance from each mark to the first point.

Step 9: From equation #1 find the average change in velocity between each point or mark on your ticker tape using the following equation:

$$\bar{v} = \frac{\Delta d}{\Delta t}$$

$$\bar{v}_{0,1} = \frac{\Delta d_{0,1}}{\Delta t_{0,1}} \qquad \bar{v}_{1,2} = \frac{\Delta d_{1,2}}{\Delta t_{1,2}} \qquad \bar{v}_{2,3} = \frac{\Delta d_{2,3}}{\Delta t_{2,3}}$$

Record as change in velocity at mark $v_{0,1}$, $v_{1,2}$, $v_{2,3}$, ... v_n.

Step 10: Calculate the acceleration using formula #2 and record as follows:

$$\bar{a} = \frac{\Delta v}{\Delta t} \qquad \bar{a}_{0,1} = \frac{\bar{v}_1 - \bar{v}_0}{\Delta t_{0,1}}$$

$$\bar{a}_{1,2} = \frac{\bar{v}_2 - \bar{v}_1}{\Delta t_{1,2}} \qquad \bar{a}_{2,3} = \frac{\bar{v}_3 - \bar{v}_2}{\Delta t_{2,3}}$$

Record as acceleration between marks as
$a_{0,1}$, $a_{1,2}$, $a_{2,3}$, ... a_n.

Motion

THESE DOTS ARE EVENLY SPACED, SHOWING A CONSTANT VELOCITY, WHERE V EQUALS DISTANCE DIVIDED BY TIME, OR V = D/t !!

Graphing the results

You will now graph your data in order to learn from your results. In each of the following graphs attempt to draw a "best fit" line. If data is widely scattered do not attempt to connect each dot but instead draw the best line you can that represents the shape of the dots. If you have access to a computer you can use a spread sheet like Microsoft Excel to plot your data.

1. Graph **Total Distance** on the vertical axis and **Total Time** on the horizontal.

2. Graph **Velocity Final** at each point on the vertical axis and **Total Time** on the horizontal.

3. Graph **Acceleration** on the vertical axis and **Total Time** on the horizontal.

Analysis

1. Identify the time intervals where your vehicle had the maximum positive and negative acceleration. Where did your vehicle have the most constant acceleration?

2. What was the vehicle's maximum speed over the timing distance and at what point did this occur?

3. How far was your vehicle pulled by the string? From the graph is it possible to determine when the string was no longer pulling the vehicle? Explain.

4. Compare your performance to the performance of other vehicles in the class and discuss how yours relates.

Surface Friction

MOTION

FRICTION

A ball rolling across the floor will eventually slows to a stop. The reason the ball slows to a stop is because of **friction**. Friction is a force that always opposes motion in a direction that is opposite to the motion of the object. An object that slides to the right experiences friction towards the left. If it was not for friction, the ball would roll forever, as long as there was nothing—like a wall—to stop its motion. Your mouse-trap car is affected by friction in the same way as the rolling ball, friction will slow it to a stop. Friction will occur anytime two surfaces slip, slide, or move against one another. There are two basic types of friction—**surface friction** and **fluid friction**. In some situations fluid friction is called air resistance. A ball falling through the air is affected by fluid friction and a block sliding on a table is mainly affected by surface friction as well as a little air resistance. **The greater the amount of friction between two surfaces, the larger the force that will be required to keep an object moving**. In order to overcome friction, a constant force is needed. In order to maintain a constant force, there must be a supply of **energy**. A ball which is given an initial push will roll until all its energy is consumed by friction, at which point it will roll to a stop. The smaller the forces

CHEESE

TABLE

Friction

of friction acting against a moving object (like a ball or mouse-trap car), the farther it will travel on its available energy supply. **Eliminating all forms of friction is the key to success no matter what type of vehicle you are building.**

Surface friction occurs between any two surfaces that touch or rub against one another. The cause of surface friction is mutual contact of irregularities between the touching surfaces. The irregularities act as obstructions to motion. Even surfaces that appear to be very smooth are irregular when viewed microscopically. Luckily, during motion surface friction is **unaffected by the relative speed** of an object; even though the speed of an object may increase, the force of surface friction will remain constant. This means that the same force is required to slide an object at a slow or fast rate of speed on a given surface. **The amount of friction acting between two surfaces depends on the kinds of material from which the two surfaces are made and how hard the surfaces are pressed together**. Ice is more slippery than concrete; therefore, ice has less friction or less resistance to slippage. A heavier brick is harder to push and has more friction than a lighter brick only because the heavier brick pushes into the ground with more force or weight.

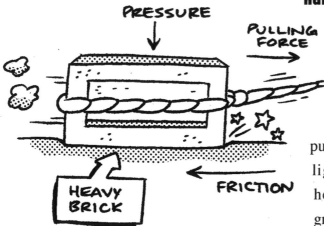

Friction

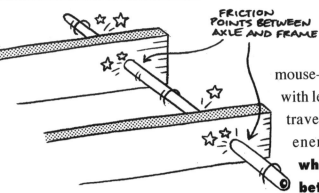

FRICTION POINTS BETWEEN AXLE AND FRAME

Minimizing surface friction on a mouse-trap car allows its wheels to spin with less resistance, resulting in a car that travels faster, farther and wastes less energy. **The most common area where surface friction will occur is between the axle and the chassis.**

The interface between the axle and the chassis is called the **bearing**. A **plain bearing** can be as simple as an axle turning in a drilled hole. A **bushing** is a smooth sleeve placed in a hole that gives the axle a smother rubbing surface, which means less surface friction. Some combinations of material should not be used because they do not help the cause; for example, avoid using aluminum as the axle or a bearing sleeve.

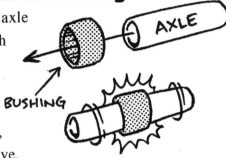

AXLE

BUSHING

A **ball bearing** is a set of balls in the hole which is arranged so that the axle rolls on the balls instead of sliding in a sleeve. A rolling ball has very little friction; therefore, ball bearings usually provide the best performance. Ball bearings have the least friction, but they are the most expensive, so you must evaluate your budget when thinking about ball bearings. You can buy small ball bearings at a local hobby store that deals with remote-controlled vehicles.

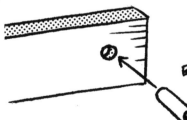

BUSHING COLLAR

ROLLER BALLS

BALL BEARING

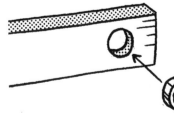

BALL BEARING

Friction

14

Construction Tip

Mounting a Ball Bearing

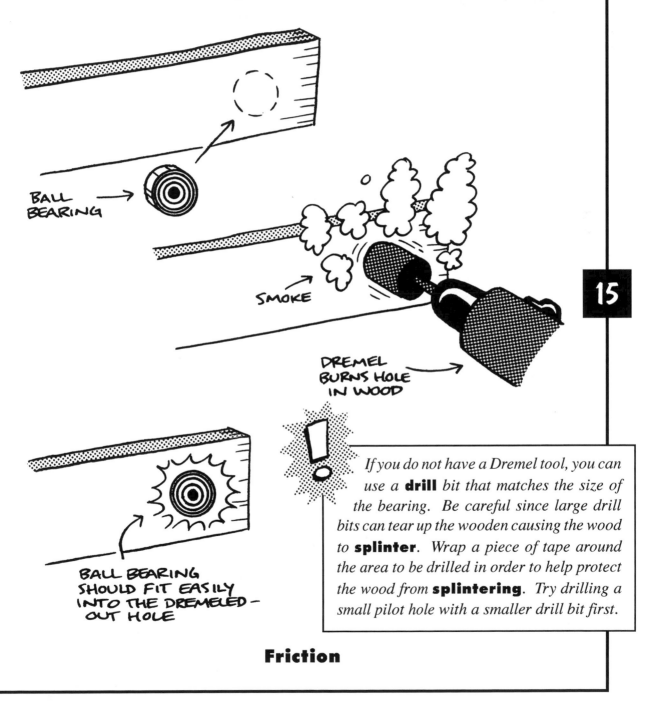

BALL BEARING

SMOKE

DREMEL BURNS HOLE IN WOOD

BALL BEARING SHOULD FIT EASILY INTO THE DREMELED-OUT HOLE

*If you do not have a Dremel tool, you can use a **drill** bit that matches the size of the bearing. Be careful since large drill bits can tear up the wooden causing the wood to **splinter**. Wrap a piece of tape around the area to be drilled in order to help protect the wood from **splintering**. Try drilling a small pilot hole with a smaller drill bit first.*

15

Friction

Adding Ball Bearings

Fixing an Axle and Bearing Mismatch

Ball Bearings are designed to reduce friction between the axle and the frame where they are in contact with one another (friction points). Bearings reduce energy loss. By adding bearings your car will travel further and faster depending on the type of car you are building.

Ball bearings are manufactured too much higher standard than the axles; therefore, a bearing may fit one 3/16 inch brass tube may not another of same diameter. Sometimes you may have to "turn" your brass tube so that it will fit with a bearing. **DO NOT FORCE BEARINGS ONTO AN AXLE**, this can wreck the bearing.

The best method for correcting small size differences between axles and bearings is to place your axle in a drill. Using 32-400 grit WET sand paper, turn the drill on and apply light pressure to the axle with the sand paper and sand away a layer of the axle. As the drill rotates hold the sandpaper around the axle and moving it along the length of the tubing. Stop often and test-fit the bearing onto the axle, once the bearing slides down the length of the axle you no longer need to turn the axle down. The sandpaper will become HOT so do not put to much pressure in one spot or you may burn your fingers.

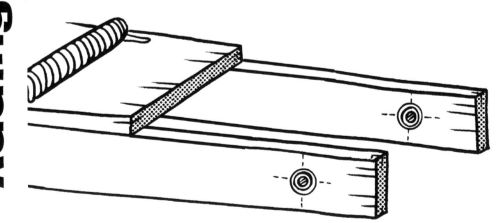

Friction

16

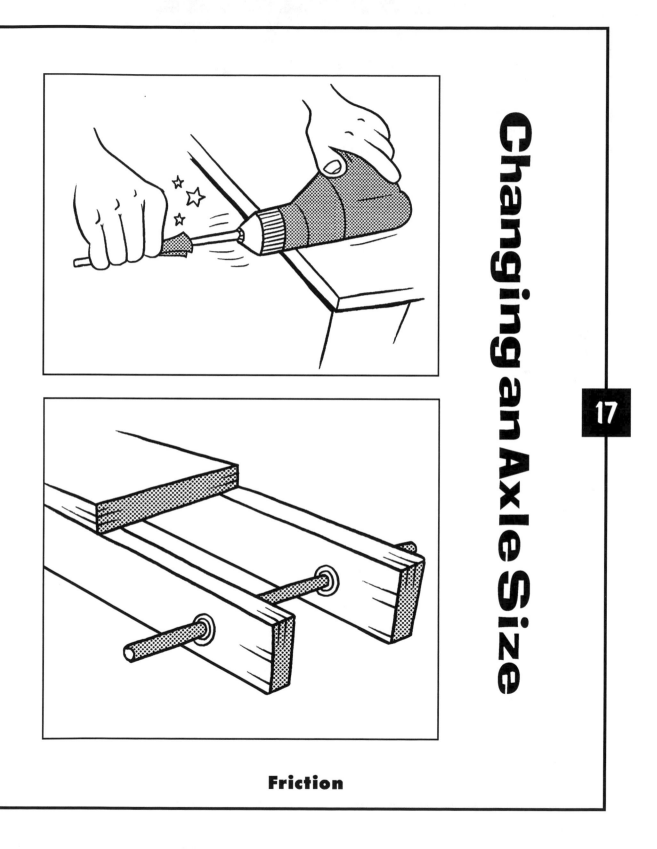

Friction

Construction Tip

Making A Bushing

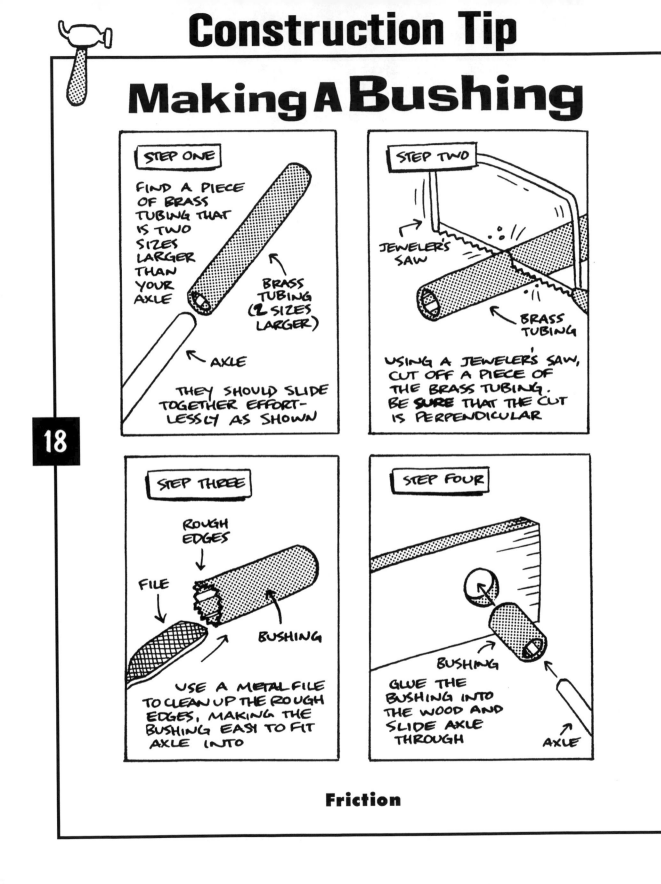

STEP ONE

FIND A PIECE OF BRASS TUBING THAT IS TWO SIZES LARGER THAN YOUR AXLE

BRASS TUBING (2 SIZES LARGER)

AXLE

THEY SHOULD SLIDE TOGETHER EFFORT-LESSLY AS SHOWN

STEP TWO

JEWELER'S SAW

BRASS TUBING

USING A JEWELER'S SAW, CUT OFF A PIECE OF THE BRASS TUBING. BE **SURE** THAT THE CUT IS PERPENDICULAR

STEP THREE

ROUGH EDGES

FILE

BUSHING

USE A METAL FILE TO CLEAN UP THE ROUGH EDGES, MAKING THE BUSHING EASY TO FIT AXLE INTO

STEP FOUR

BUSHING

GLUE THE BUSHING INTO THE WOOD AND SLIDE AXLE THROUGH

AXLE

Friction

Construction Tip

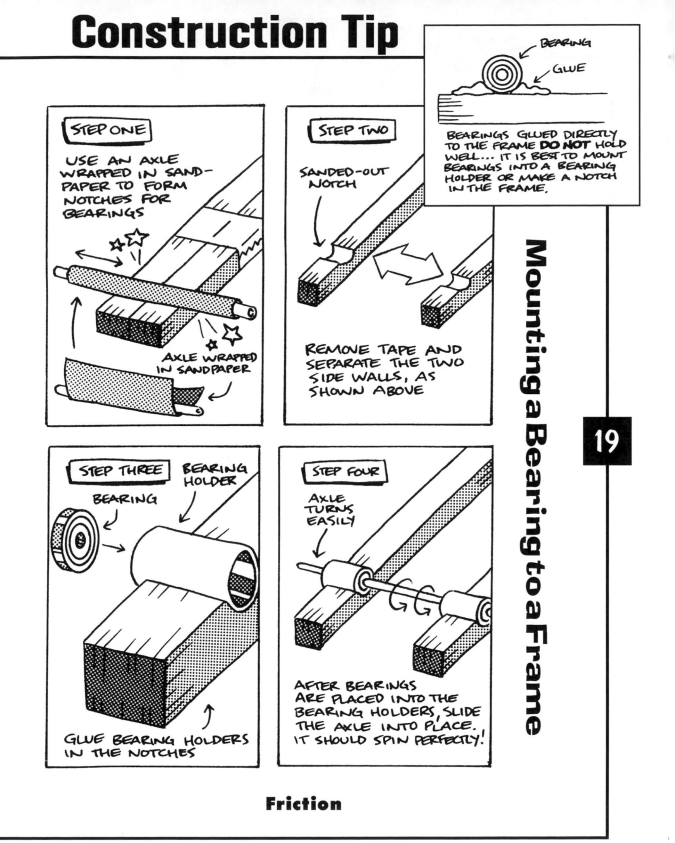

BEARING

GLUE

BEARINGS GLUED DIRECTLY TO THE FRAME **DO NOT** HOLD WELL... IT IS BEST TO MOUNT BEARINGS INTO A BEARING HOLDER OR MAKE A NOTCH IN THE FRAME.

STEP ONE

USE AN AXLE WRAPPED IN SAND-PAPER TO FORM NOTCHES FOR BEARINGS

AXLE WRAPPED IN SANDPAPER

STEP TWO

SANDED-OUT NOTCH

REMOVE TAPE AND SEPARATE THE TWO SIDE WALLS, AS SHOWN ABOVE

STEP THREE

BEARING HOLDER

BEARING

GLUE BEARING HOLDERS IN THE NOTCHES

STEP FOUR

AXLE TURNS EASILY

AFTER BEARINGS ARE PLACED INTO THE BEARING HOLDERS, SLIDE THE AXLE INTO PLACE. IT SHOULD SPIN PERFECTLY!

Mounting a Bearing to a Frame

19

Friction

For an object spinning against another object, like an axle turning inside the frame of a mouse-trap car, the **surface friction** is complicated by torque, which will be discussed in another part of this book. A thicker diameter axle or bearing will stop turning sooner than a comparable thinner axle or smaller bearing. The reason is as follows: The force of friction is the same around the surface of a large and small diameter axle but the location of where the force of friction is being applied from the center of the rotating axle is not the same. With a larger diameter axle, the frictional force is applied further from the center of rotation than with the smaller diameter axle. Torque is a combination of an applied force and the location of that force from the point of rotation. The further from the point of rotation, the greater the torque becomes for the same size force. Smaller diameter axles and bearings translate into less stopping torque and better performance. A pressure bearing or even a magnetic bearing where only the sharpened tip of the axle touches the bearing is the best solution to beating friction.

20

LARGE AXLE

MORE FRICTION

SMALL AXLE

LESS FRICTION

Friction

Lubrications help moving parts slide against each other with less energy loss by reducing the surface friction. Try a quick experiment. Rub your hands together lightly and quickly. You should notice that your hands become warm, this is because the friction between your hands turns some of the input energy into heat. Heat is often lost or wasted energy in many moving machines. Put a small amount of hand lotion onto your hands and try the experiment again. Notice that your hands do not become as hot and it is easier to move them against one another. Different **lubricants** work better with different materials. Oils and greases are used between most metal-on-metal parts. Oils do not work well between metal-on-wood parts, but graphite powder is an excellent friction reducer. It is always best to try different lubricants and observe their effects. WD-40®, Dura-Lube®, Slick 50®, and graphite are necessary materials for your tool box.

Brain Tip

A SECRET TIP FROM DOC FIZZIX: *Do not use lubricants with ball bearings. Soak ball bearings in WD-40 in order to remove all grease residue from within the bearing. Although lubricants prevent wear and in some cases reduce the overall force of friction, with slow moving mouse-trap cars lubricants actually increase the friction. The reason that lubricants do not work well at low speeds has to do with the cohesive forces of the lubricant. At low speeds lubricants are actually sticky and stick to themselves, requiring larger forces to break free and move.*

SPIN A BEARING ON A PENCIL TO REMOVE GREASE AFTER SOAKING IN ALCOHOL

Friction

Friction is not restricted to solids sliding over one another, friction also occurs in liquids and gases, collectively called **fluids**. Just as the friction between surface friction depends on the nature of the surfaces, **fluid friction** depends on the nature of the fluid. For example, friction is greater in water than it is in air. But unlike the surface friction, fluid friction **depends on speed and area of contact**. This makes

sense, for the amount of fluid pushed aside by a boat or airplane depends on the size and the shape of the craft. A slow-moving boat or airplane encounters less friction than fast-moving boats or airplanes. Wide boats and airplanes must push aside more fluid than narrower crafts. If the flow of fluid is relatively smooth, the friction force is approximately proportional to the speed of the object. Above a

A TEAR DROP IS THE MOST AERODYNAMIC SHAPE, CUTTING THROUGH THE AIR WITH THE LEAST AMOUNT OF AIR RESISTANCE, MUCH LIKE THE WING OF AN AIRPLANE.

critical speed this simple proportion breaks down as fluid flow becomes erratic and friction increases dramatically.

The amount of air friction or fluid friction depends on the speed and the shape of a moving object. The faster an object moves, the more collisions that occur with particles of the fluid, causing increased friction. The shape of a moving object, its **aerodynamic,** determines the **ease of flow** of the fluid around the moving object. Fast cars are designed and shaped to cut through the air with less friction so they can move faster. Trucks have a special cowling that increases their aerodynamics and allows air to flow more easily over the trailer. Increased aerodynamics saves energy. Fish have aerodynamic shapes that allow them to move through the water with less effort. Keep in mind that there are situations in which you would want to increase the air resistance. A good example is the use of a parachute on a dragster to help it stop the vehicle or the flaps on an airplane to help slow it down.

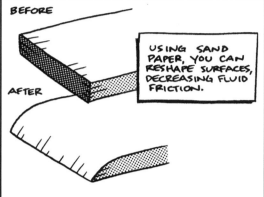

Because the force of **air resistance** increases as the speed of an object increases, faster moving mouse-trap cars will have more air resistance acting against them, causing them to use more energy and come to rest sooner than a similarly built slower-moving mouse-trap car. Keeping this in mind, good aerodynamics will improve performance of any vehicle, no matter what type of car you are building. This means that your car must be smooth with few points of **air drag**. Inspect the body for flat surfaces on leading edges that could catch air, thus increasing the air drag. Rounding the leading edges of your vehicle will allow for smoother movement of air around your vehicle. Cars made from wood need to be sanded smooth. **Sanding** will remove any unwanted irregularities, thus decreasing the force of air resistance acting on your car once it is in motion. Tires should be thin. Thin tires are more aerodynamic and slice through the air more smoothly. Wider tires will have more air drag than narrower tires. Therefore, try to pick thin tires when you are building your mouse-trap car.

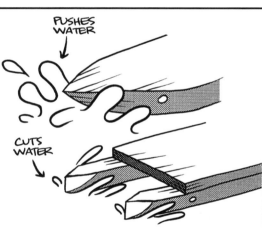

The two side runners of the bottom boat reduce the surface area and the fluid friction over the top boat's big hull.

Friction

Experiment

24

To see how much force the air can have, try the following **experiment** next time you are in a car. Carefully hold your hand out the window. Try holding your hand so that your thumb points toward the sky and then try holding your hand so that your thumb point towards the direction of travel. You will have a better understanding of **fluid friction** after this experiment.

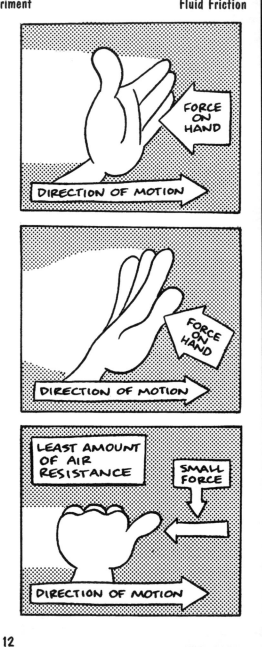

12

Friction

Construction Tip
Thrust Washers

Thrust washers can be used to eliminate the rubbing friction of a wheel touching the frame. If a wheel has a side-to-side movement and touches the frame, a metal washer can be used to prevent the wheel from directly touching the frame, which will causing poor performance of your vehicle In these pictures, a rubber stopper is placed on the axle to help eliminate the side-to-side movement and then a metal washer is placed between the frame and the stopper.

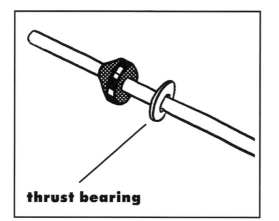

thrust bearing

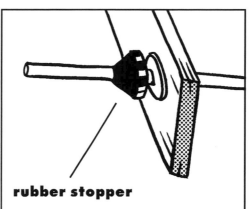

rubber stopper

Experiment

Try an experiment to learn about a **thrust bearing**. *Place a book on the table and give it a spin. The book should spin slowly and then stop quickly. Now place a coin under the book and give it a spin again. The book should spin for a considerably longer time before stopping.*

PENNY IS PLACED UNDERNEATH BOOK

Friction

Purpose
To determine the amount of rolling friction acting against your mousetrap car and the coefficient of friction.

Materials
Ruler (A caliper works better for smaller measurements.)
Smooth Ramp
Tape Measure

Variables needed from other labs
Total Potential Energy from Lab #5

Discussion
Friction is a force that acts against the motion of all moving objects. Energy is required to overcome friction and keep an object moving. Mousetrap cars start with a limited supply of energy. This energy is used to overcome friction and propel the vehicle. The less friction acting against a moving mousetrap car, the less energy that is consumed to friction and the further that the vehicle will travel. A moving mousetrap car is affected by two type of friction: airfriction and bearing friction. Airfriction is a large factor only with cars that are moving fast and is nearly negligible for slow-moving distance cars; therefore, in this lab you will only take bearing friction into consideration. Bearing friction is actually caused by two surfaces rubbing against one another. The amount of friction depends on the materials that are doing the rubbing and the force pressing them together (Formula #3). In this lab you will find the combined force of friction from all bearings on your vehicle. This combined frictional force will be called the rolling friction. The smaller the coefficient of friction, the more efficient your mousetrap car and the greater the travel distance will be.

Rolling Friction

The Set-up

Finding the theoretical rolling friction requires placing your mousetrap car on a smooth and flat board or ramp. The ramp will be elevated from one end slowly until your mousetrap car "JUST" begins to roll at constant velocity. This point or angle is where the force pulling the car down the ramp is equal to the force of rolling friction acting against the car (Formula #2). The force pulling the car down the ramp is a combination of two forces: the force of gravity pulling straight down and the normal force of the ramp pushing back (Formula #4). As the angle of the ramp is increased, the normal force decreases (Formula #5). The force of gravity remains unchanged for all angles. The difference between the two forces causes the force down the ramp to increase. The greater the angle required to move the car, the more friction there will be acting against the car's motion. The angle is directly proportional to the force of friction or the coefficient of rolling friction. **LOWER ANGLES** are more desirable (Formula #7).

27

$F_d = F_f$

How it Works:
The force pulling the vehicle down the ramp is equal to the force of friction acting against the car AS LONG as the mousetrap car moves down the ramp at a constant velocity. In some cases, once the vehicle starts to move the ramp has to be lowered in order to maintain constant velocity.

Rolling Friction

Formulas

Formula #1: $\Sigma F = 0$

The sum of all forces must equal "zero" if there is no acceleration.

Formula #2: $\text{Force}_{\text{Pulling}} = \text{Force}_{\text{of friction}}$

Formula #3: $f_{rf} = \mu N$

Force of friction is equal to the coefficient of friction times the normal force

$$\sin \theta = \frac{h}{L}$$

Because your measurements are from a slope, you will have to use some trigonometry

Formula #4: $f_{rf} = \sin\theta \cdot w$

The force down an angled ramp is equal to the force of friction as long as the vehicle rolls down the ramp with a constant velocity.

Formula #5: $N = \cos\theta \cdot w$

The normal force is the force that is perpendicular to the angled ramp.

Formula #6: $\mu = \dfrac{\sin\theta \cdot w}{\cos\theta \cdot w} = \tan\theta$

Resolving for the coefficient of friction from Formulas #3, #4 and #5

Formula #7: $\mu = \tan\theta$

The coefficient of friction

Rolling Friction

Trigonometry

Trigonometry is a fancy type of mathematics that is based on simple relationships of all right triangles. Ancient mathematicians found that all right triangles are proportional by ratios of their sides and angles. These ratios times the angle are known as sine, cosine, and tangent. Knowing one of the angles other than the right angle-and any one of the sides to the triangle-will allow you can calculate everything else you would ever need to know about that triangle's sides or angles.

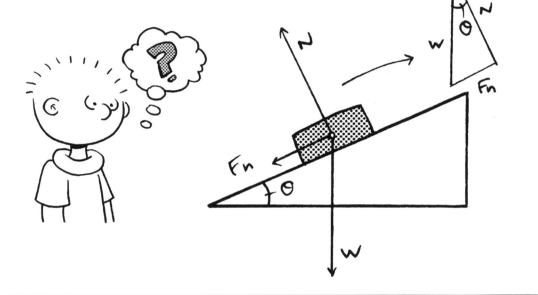

How it Works

The angle of the ramp in this experiment forms a right triangle. The force due to gravity and the normal force of the ramp's surface cause a force directed down the ramp called "Force Down." These three forces form a right triangle which has the same angle as the base of the ramp. Knowing the angle of the base of the ramp and the weight of the car on the ramp, we can solve for any other force including the force acting down the ramp and which is equal to the force of friction.

Rolling Friction

Let The Good Times Roll

Step 1: Start by selecting a long and smooth board or ramp that will not bend or flex when lifted at one end. Your vehicle must fit on the ramp.

Step 2: Measure the length of the board and record this measurement as the board length (L).

Step 3: Place your vehicle on the ramp and begin lifting by one end. Slowly lift until the vehicle "JUST" begins to roll. Measure carefully and accurately the elevation of the board when the vehicle begins to roll and record this in the data table as the height (h). Repeat this process 5 to 10 times for more accurate results. (Note: You must subtract the thickness of the board from the height. Measure both ends of the ramp to correctly calculate the height.)

Data Table #1

Trial #	Board Length (m)	Raised Height (m)	Angle	Coefficient of Rolling Friction	Friction (N)	Starting Energy (J)	Predicted Travel Distance
1	L=	$h_1=$	$\theta_1=$	$\mu_1=$	$f_1=$	PE=	$d_1=$
2	L=	$h_2=$	$\theta_2=$	$\mu_2=$	$f_2=$	PE=	$d_2=$
3	L=	$h_3=$	$\theta_3=$	$\mu_3=$	$f_3=$	PE=	$d_3=$
4	L=	$h_4=$	$\theta_4=$	$\mu_4=$	$f_4=$	PE=	$d_4=$
AVE		h=	$\theta=$	$\mu=$	f=		d=

Rolling Friction

Step 4: Calculate the angle for each trial using the following equation:

$$\theta = \frac{h}{L} \sin^{-1}$$

Step 5: From the derived formula, calculate the coefficient of friction for each trial. The coefficient of friction is directly proportional to the angle of the ramp. Smaller angles translate into greater travel distance.

$$\mu = \tan\theta$$

Step 6: If this lab is performed correctly, the force of rolling friction acting against your car is equal to the force pulling the vehicle down the ramp in the elevated state. Calculate the force of friction by assuming that the force down the ramp is equal to the force of friction acting against the motion of your vehicle. Solve for the force down the ramp. MAKE SURE to use the weight of your vehicle in Newtons. If you have the mass in kilograms, you can calculate the weight by multiplying the mass of your vehicle by 9.8 m/s^2 or find the weight by weighing your vehicle on a spring scale.

$$f_{rf} = \sin\theta \cdot w$$

Step 7: Using the starting energy that you calculated in Lab #4 you can calculate the predicted travel distance by using the following:

$$\text{Predicted Travel Distance} = \frac{\text{Total Potential Energy}}{\text{Rolling Friction}}$$

Rolling Friction

The number of wheels your vehicle has does not have an effect on the overall friction. Vehicles with three wheels will often have fewer friction points than vehicles with four wheels. However, the **distribution of weight** for a three wheeled vehicle is spread out over three wheels rather than four; therefore, there is more pressure on the turning points and an increase in friction for each point. The decease in the number of **friction points** is offset by the increase in **pressure**. This is what we call "a wash." You get no change! No matter the number of wheels, the total amount of friction should be the same. The advantage of using fewer wheels is better wheel alignment. With three-wheeled cars, it will be easier to adjust the steering of the vehicle because there are fewer wheels to be aligned.

MOST
ENERGY
EFFICIENT

ENERGY
LOST

FRICTION
CAUSES
TURN

32

Steering Alignment

Building a vehicle that travels straight can be somewhat challenging, especially when building a long traveling distance vehicle where any small misalignment in the wheels is exaggerated over a long distance. If your car does not travel straight, energy is being wasted. Vehicles turn because of one reason: **"THE WHEELS ARE NOT POINTING IN THE SAME DIRECTION!"** What does wheel alignment have to do with friction? Vehicles turn because wheels use friction to push a vehicle into a turn. For example, if a wheel is turned so that it points to the left, the ground actually pushes the car in this direction. If the frictional force is not large enough to overcome the **momentum** of the vehicle (like a car traveling fast

Friction

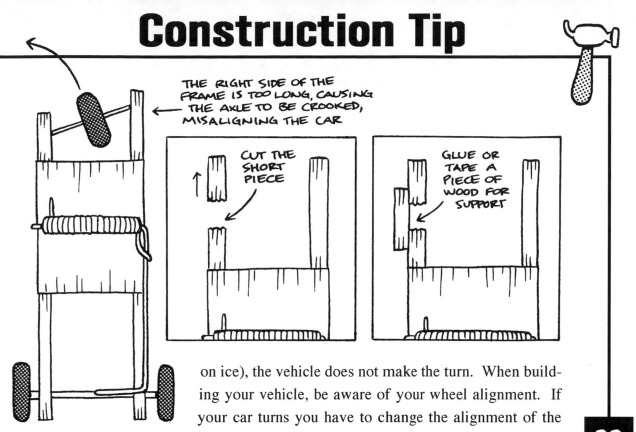

THE RIGHT SIDE OF THE FRAME IS TOO LONG, CAUSING THE AXLE TO BE CROOKED, MISALIGNING THE CAR

CUT THE SHORT PIECE

GLUE OR TAPE A PIECE OF WOOD FOR SUPPORT

on ice), the vehicle does not make the turn. When building your vehicle, be aware of your wheel alignment. If your car turns you have to change the alignment of the wheels in the direction opposite the turn. Sometimes on a big-wheeled vehicle the **string tension** can pull an axle out of alignment, so always test your car under operating conditions. **Do not just push your vehicle to see if it travels straight.**

33

Another Idea to Get You Going Straight

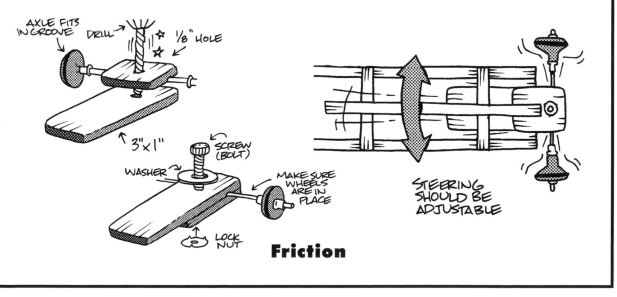

AXLE FITS IN GROOVE

DRILL

1/8" HOLE

3"x1"

WASHER

SCREW (BOLT)

MAKE SURE WHEELS ARE IN PLACE

LOCK NUT

Friction

STEERING SHOULD BE ADJUSTABLE

Wheel Size

You should consider the **diameter** of the wheels in the construction of your distance vehicle. The number of turns a wheel makes has an effect on the energy consumed by a wheel. Large diameter wheels will make fewer turns over the same distance compared to smaller diameter wheels, thus reducing the total amount of energy needed to overcome friction.

Larger wheels do not decrease the *amount* of friction, only *how far* the friction acts. **Energy**, or **work**, is equal to the force times the distance over which the force is applied. If the force of friction is applied over a smaller turning distance compared to vehicle travel distance, less energy will be wasted due to friction, which leaves more energy to move the car.

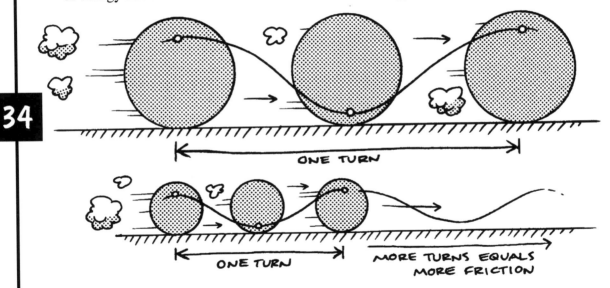

ONE TURN

ONE TURN

MORE TURNS EQUALS MORE FRICTION

With distance vehicles, you want the smallest possible force acting over the longest possible distance; therefore, you want to build a car with a small axle to a large wheel ratio. A small axle with a large wheel will cover more distance per each turn of the axle when compared to a smaller wheel size with the same axle.

Friction

Construction Tip

Making a Big Wheel

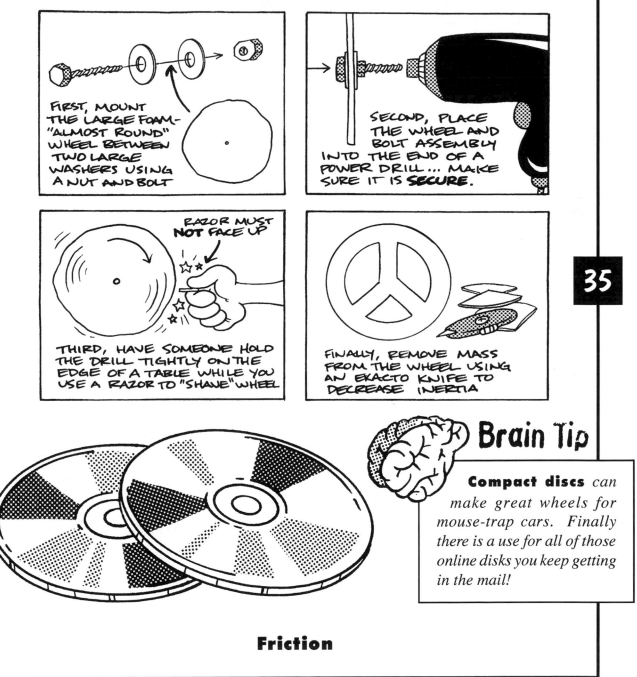

FIRST, MOUNT THE LARGE FOAM "ALMOST ROUND" WHEEL BETWEEN TWO LARGE WASHERS USING A NUT AND BOLT

SECOND, PLACE THE WHEEL AND BOLT ASSEMBLY INTO THE END OF A POWER DRILL... MAKE SURE IT IS **SECURE.**

RAZOR MUST **NOT FACE UP**

THIRD, HAVE SOMEONE HOLD THE DRILL TIGHTLY ON THE EDGE OF A TABLE WHILE YOU USE A RAZOR TO "SHAVE" WHEEL

FINALLY, REMOVE MASS FROM THE WHEEL USING AN EKACTO KNIFE TO DECREASE INERTIA

Brain Tip

Compact discs *can make great wheels for mouse-trap cars. Finally there is a use for all of those online disks you keep getting in the mail!*

Friction

Friction is not always a bad thing. **Without friction you could not move anywhere**. As you walk forward, it is the friction on the bottom of your feet that allows for the grip you need to move. It is the friction between the road and your tires that keeps the wheels from slipping and allows your vehicle to move. This type of friction is called **traction** and is a desired form of friction. What type of wheels work best: fat tires, thin tires, knobby tires, or smooth tires? Knobby tires have good traction if the road surface is rough, but the trade-off is that they are inefficient and use more energy than smooth wheels. When pressure is placed directly on a

KNOB

TIRE

COMPRESSED KNOBS
APPLY EXTRA PRESSURE
WHICH GENERATES MORE
HEAT, WASTING ENERGY

knob, more force compresses the tire causing the rubber and air inside the tire to heat up. The energy it takes to compress the rubber and air in the tire is lost as heat. Knobby tires become hotter with continued use. Race cars use smooth tires called **slicks**. Smooth wheels will be more energy efficient and allow a car to travel faster. On mouse-trap cars, smooth tires will allow a vehicle to travel a longer distance.

The amount of **grip** your tires have on the floor not only depends on whether you have knobby tires or slicks but also depends on the material your tires are made from and the force pushing the tires to the floor. Different compounds of

TRACTION
ACTION™

36

Friction

materials will have different amounts of grip. For instance, rubber bands wrapped around a wooden wheel will provide better grip during acceleration than the wood of the wheel will alone. **You should select or design tires to provide maximum traction or grip on the floor**. Tires with little grip on

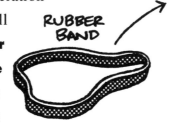

RUBBER BAND

the floor will have a tendency to slip when under a load, thereby decreasing your car's maximum acceleration or distance. You can also increase the traction by adding a non-slipping gel like **Traction Action**®, a sticky gel that is smeared on the wheels. Experiment with different materials in order to find the best traction.

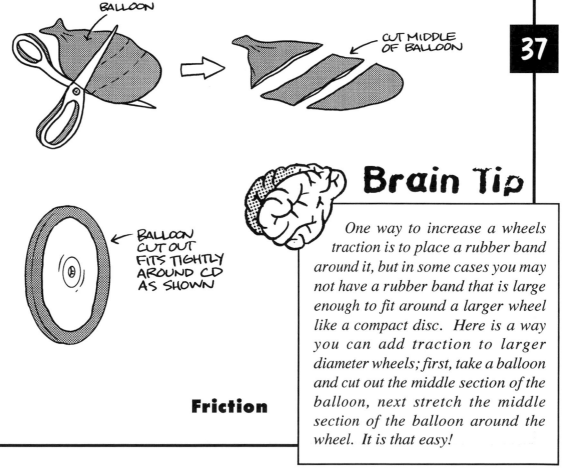

BALLOON

CUT MIDDLE OF BALLOON

BALLOON CUT OUT FITS TIGHTLY AROUND CD AS SHOWN

Friction

Brain Tip

One way to increase a wheels traction is to place a rubber band around it, but in some cases you may not have a rubber band that is large enough to fit around a larger wheel like a compact disc. Here is a way you can add traction to larger diameter wheels; first, take a balloon and cut out the middle section of the balloon, next stretch the middle section of the balloon around the wheel. It is that easy!

Lab #3- The Spinning Wheels

Purpose

To determine the amount of grip or traction your drive wheels have on the floor.

Materials

  spring scale or force probe
  string
  tape to lock wheels

Discussion

If your vehicle does not have enough grip on the floor AND you have too much pulling force your wheels will spin-out! The more "grip" or traction your wheels have on the floor surface, the greater the acceleration that is possible for your vehicle. If you are making a speed-trap or a power pulling vehicle you want to test different materials on your wheels to make sure you have the maximum traction possible; for example, rubber balloons on wheels, rubber bands on wheels, different compounds, etc. Once you have found the maximum traction, you can adjust the length of your mousetrap's lever arm in order to achieve the greatest possible pulling force. Shorter lever arms have greater force for more power or acceleration for your vehicle. Keep in mind that the amount of traction will vary from surface to surface because not all surfaces have the same grip. Example, your car will have more grip on concrete than on ice; because of this, you must test your vehicle's traction on the actual course where you will be running your contest or activity. In this activity you will find that actual for of traction and the coefficient of friction between your vehicles drive wheels and the floor. The coefficient of friction tells you how slippery two surfaces are together. The larger the coefficient of friction, the more grip or traction your vehicle will have with that surface.

Rolling Friction

Formulas

Formula #1: $\Sigma F = 0$

The sum of all forces must equal "zero" if there is no acceleration.

Formula #2:   Force Pulling = Force of Traction

Formula #3: $f_{rf} = \mu N$

The force of traction or friction is equal to the coefficient of friction times the normal force or the force the drive wheels press on the floor.

Step 1: With a piece of tape lock the drive wheel(s) to prevent them from turning. The non-drive wheels should be aloud to turn freely.

Step 2: Attach a sensitive spring scale or force probe to the front of the car. It is best to tie a string to the front of that car and then attach the spring scale to the string.

Step 3: Pull the vehicle on the race surface at an even force and CONSTANT speed keeping the scale or force probe parallel to the road. Pull the vehicle several time and record the readings each time calculating an average. The force required to drag your car is equal to the force of traction, calculate the average and record.

Step 4: To find the coefficient of friction between the drive wheels and the floor you need to attach the spring scale to the drive axle and lift directly up until the drive wheels just lift off the table. Record this number as the force on the drive wheels. Using the formulas, divide the force of traction by the force on the drive wheels

$$\mu = \frac{f}{N}$$

Rolling Friction

Newton's First Law of Motion:

Every material object continues in its state of rest or in uniform motion in a straight line unless it is compelled to change that state by forces acting on it.

40

Inertia is just a fancy word that means **resistance to change**. **Mass** is the numerical measurement of inertia. **Weight** is related to mass and inertia but weight is not the same thing. Weight is a product of the amount of mass an object has and the amount of gravity pulling on the mass. An example of the difference can be understood using a bowling ball. On earth you can feel the weight of a bowling ball as you hold it to your side. If you held the bowling ball on the moon, it would feel a lot lighter than on the earth. This is because the gravity on the moon is not as strong as the gravity on the earth; therefore, the weight of the bowling ball is less than its weight on the earth. Now if you compared throwing the bowling ball down the bowling lane on the earth and on the moon you would find that there is no apparent difference in force or feel. This is because the mass of the bowling ball is the same in each location and by throwing the bowling ball you are working against its inertia—not its weight.

Inertia, Force, Acceleration

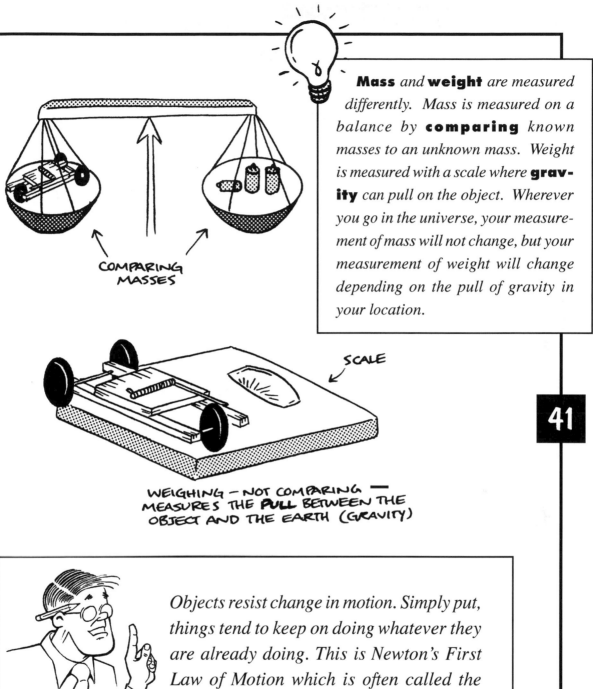

Mass and **weight** are measured differently. Mass is measured on a balance by **comparing** known masses to an unknown mass. Weight is measured with a scale where **gravity** can pull on the object. Wherever you go in the universe, your measurement of mass will not change, but your measurement of weight will change depending on the pull of gravity in your location.

COMPARING MASSES

SCALE

41

WEIGHING — NOT COMPARING — MEASURES THE **PULL** BETWEEN THE OBJECT AND THE EARTH (GRAVITY)

Objects resist change in motion. Simply put, things tend to keep on doing whatever they are already doing. This is Newton's First Law of Motion which is often called the **Law of Inertia**.

Inertia, Force, Acceleration

42

A good way to learn about **inertia** is the following experiment. Place some old dishes and plates on top of a smooth table cloth. With a quick tug, pull the table cloth off the table! **Do not pull up on the table cloth but pull outward**. This demonstrates that objects at rest tend to stay at rest. This experiment will work better with food on the plates and in the bowls.

TADA!

Inertia, Force, Acceleration

Newton's Second Law

If you want to change the motion of an object, you have to apply a **force**. *Net forces cause objects to accelerate or change their state of motion. Newton recognized that his first law needed some additional explanation because most of the motion we observe around us undergoes changes and is the result of one or more applied forces; therefore,* **Newton wrote a Second Law of Motion which relates force, mass, and acceleration.**

Newton's Second Law of Motion:

The acceleration of an object is directly proportional to the net force acting on the object (in the direction of the net force) and is inversely proportional to the mass of the object.

Simply put, **mass resists change or acceleration, and force causes acceleration**. If you want to double the acceleration of an object, you have to double the pulling or pushing force. If you can't increase the force and you still want to increase the acceleration, then you have to **remove mass** (e.g., cut the original mass in half if you want to double the acceleration).

Inertia, Force, Acceleration

Newton's Third Law

Newton's Third Law of Motion:

Whenever one object exerts a force on a second object, the second object exerts an equal and opposite force on the first.

In its most basic definition, a **force is a push or a pull**. Newton recognized that a force is actually an interaction between two objects. Example, when you push on the wall, the wall pushes back on you! You and the wall are an interaction pair, you apply a force to the wall and the wall applies a force back, the evidence is you bent fingers. As Newton stated in his third law of motion, **you can not push or pull on any object without that object doing the same back to you**.

44

Most often stated:

For every action there is an equal and opposite reaction.

YOU CANNOT PUSH ANY HARDER THAN SOMETHING PUSHES BACK

When you are walking, you push on the floor and the floor pushes back on you, if the floor does not push back, you can do not move. A mousetrap car is propelled because the drive wheels push on the floor and the floor push back on the car causing it to move or accelerate. A vehicle's acceleration is limited by the interaction between the wheels and

ACTION - REACTION

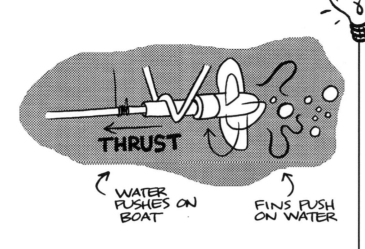

THRUST

WATER PUSHES ON BOAT

FINS PUSH ON WATER

With a boat, the propeller pushes on the water and the water pushes back on the propeller. The push of the water back on the boat creates a thrust that is similar to the thrust that is produced by the gases of a rocket engine as it push back against the rocket causing it to accelerate.

the floor. With a speed car, or any vehicle that produces a lot of torque, the wheels can only push as hard as the floor can push back. Therefore, if the floor can not push back with the same force as the wheels push, then the wheels will spin in place and the car will not accelerate to its fullest potential. Of course the trick when building a fast mousetrap powered car is to increase the tracking between the wheels and the floor so that the floor CAN push back with the maximum force that the wheels can generate with the floor.

YOU CANNOT PULL ANY HARDER THAN SOMETHING PULLS BACK

ACTION - REACTION

Newton's Laws and Building Your Car

When you build your car, Newton's laws remind you of the following: **mass is resistance to change!** Therefore, more massive vehicles will require more force and energy to start moving when compared to less massive vehicles. Whether building a speed car or distance car, **it is best to build the lightest vehicle possible**. Vehicles that are light will not only be easier to start moving but will also have less friction acting on the bearings than heavier vehicles will. Because the frame of your car rests directly on its bearings, heavier frames will press on the bearings with greater force, causing the bearings to grind more than on a lighter frame. Be careful since a car that is too light will not have enough traction to accelerate quickly. Somewhere between too heavy and too light is the perfect amount of mass for your vehicle, and only through experimentation will you find your target mass. In the process of finding your ideal mass, it is best to remove as much mass as possible because you can always add mass to strategic locations later to improve performance. Think about Newton's laws when you are building your car. **Mass works against acceleration. Remove as much mass as possible!** Force causes acceleration. If you need more pulling force, you can shorten the lever arm and move the mouse trap closer to the drive wheels. Shortening the lever arm implies moving the string closer to the hinge on the mouse-trap.

LESS FORCE

MORE FORCE

*Adjust the **pulling force** by attaching the string to different points on the lever arm. When you change the string attachment point, you must also adjust the position of the mouse-trap from the pulling axle.*

Inertia, Force, Acceleration

Construction Tip

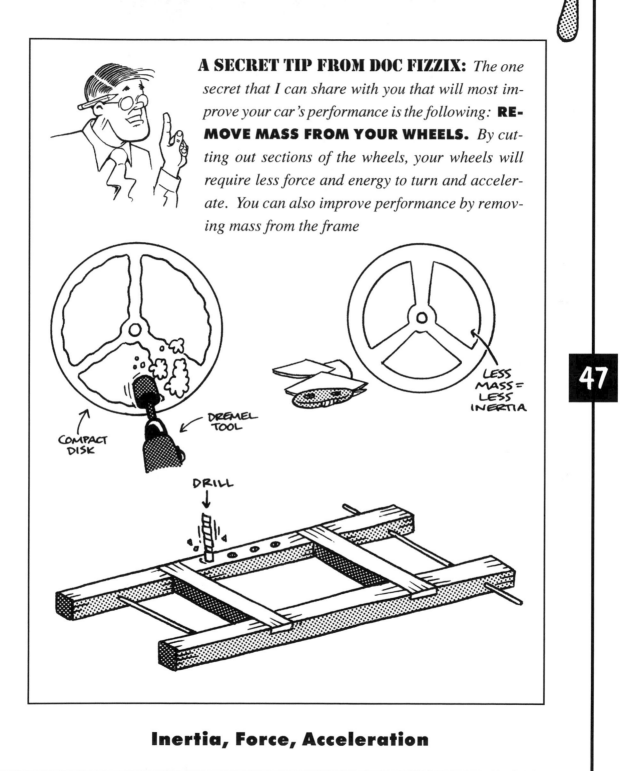

A SECRET TIP FROM DOC FIZZIX: *The one secret that I can share with you that will most improve your car's performance is the following:* **REMOVE MASS FROM YOUR WHEELS.** *By cutting out sections of the wheels, your wheels will require less force and energy to turn and accelerate. You can also improve performance by removing mass from the frame*

COMPACT DISK

DREMEL TOOL

LESS MASS = LESS INERTIA

DRILL

Inertia, Force, Acceleration

String

The mouse trap only exerts a force where you direct it to exert a force. String is often used to transfer a force from one point to another. **Choosing the proper string is critical.** If you use a string that cannot handle the pulling force, it will snap as you release the mouse trap. If you use a string that is too thick, it will not wind around the drive axle smoothly, causing the pulling force to be inconsistent. **DO NOT USE THREAD.** Use **Kevlar®**-braided fishing string, not the plastic-type fishing string. Kevlar®-braided fishing string is the best string to use because it does not stretch and can wind around a small axle without tangling. Kevlar®-braided fishing line is extremely strong and thin so that it will not break or get tangled while unwinding from the axle. The string must not be tied to the axle. If the string is tied to the axle, it will begin to rewind itself and will cause your car to come to a sudden stop. String **slippage** during the acceleration of your vehicle can be eliminated by a **hook-like device** attached to the car's axle on which a looped string or hook can be attached.

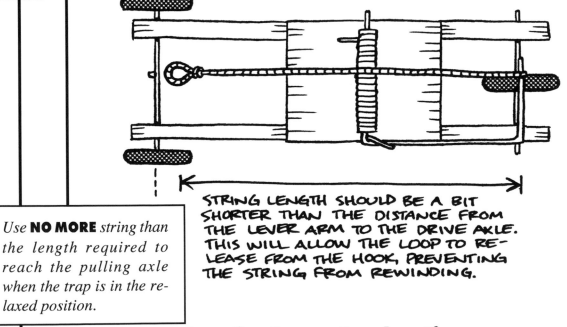

STRING LENGTH SHOULD BE A BIT SHORTER THAN THE DISTANCE FROM THE LEVER ARM TO THE DRIVE AKLE. THIS WILL ALLOW THE LOOP TO RELEASE FROM THE HOOK, PREVENTING THE STRING FROM REWINDING.

*Use **NO MORE** string than the length required to reach the pulling axle when the trap is in the relaxed position.*

Inertia, Force, Acceleration

Construction Tip

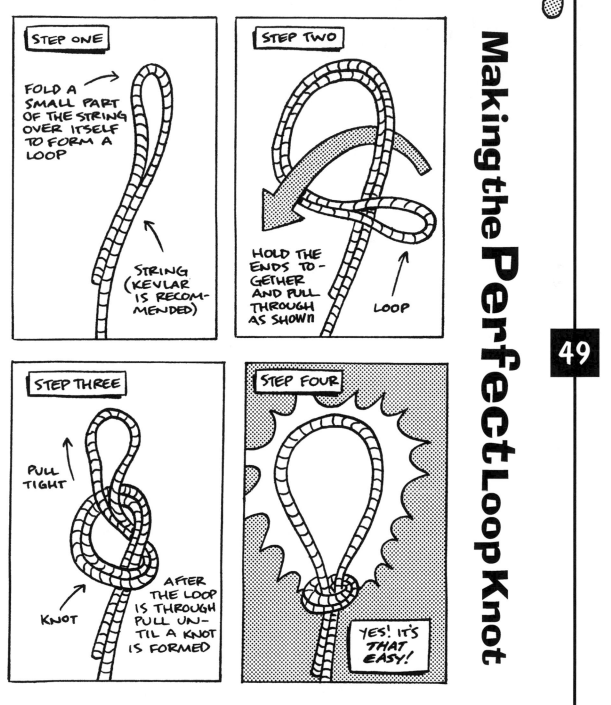

Making the Perfect Loop Knot

STEP ONE

FOLD A SMALL PART OF THE STRING OVER ITSELF TO FORM A LOOP

STRING (KEVLAR IS RECOMMENDED)

STEP TWO

HOLD THE ENDS TOGETHER AND PULL THROUGH AS SHOWN

LOOP

STEP THREE

PULL TIGHT

KNOT

AFTER THE LOOP IS THROUGH PULL UNTIL A KNOT IS FORMED

STEP FOUR

YES! IT'S *THAT* EASY!

Inertia, Force, Acceleration

Construction Tip

Making an Axle Hook

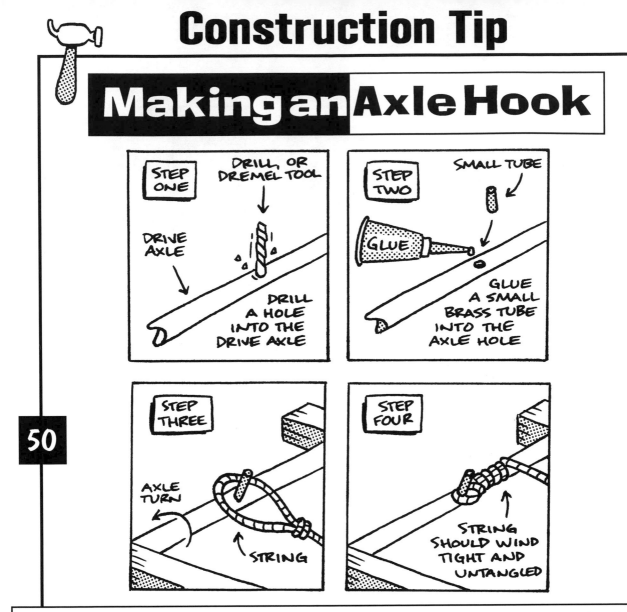

STEP ONE
DRILL, OR DREMEL TOOL
DRIVE AXLE
DRILL A HOLE INTO THE DRIVE AXLE

STEP TWO
SMALL TUBE
GLUE
GLUE A SMALL BRASS TUBE INTO THE AXLE HOLE

STEP THREE
AXLE TURN
STRING

STEP FOUR
STRING SHOULD WIND TIGHT AND UNTANGLED

In order to achieve **maximum performance** *from your mouse-trap car, it is important that the pulling string does not* **slip off** *the drive axle* **prematurely**. *A* **release hook** *can be constructed to allow the string to remain connected to the axle during the pulling phase and then release once the pulling has stopped. There are two different ways presented in this book to make a good axle hook. The first method is to drill a small hole into the drive axle and then attach a small splint to act as a hook. The second method is to wrap a small piece of wire around the drive axle, twist and glue it in place, and then trim the wire. In either example, if the hook is too long, it may snag the string and not properly release it from the drive axle.*

Inertia, Force, Acceleration

Another

Making an Axle Hook

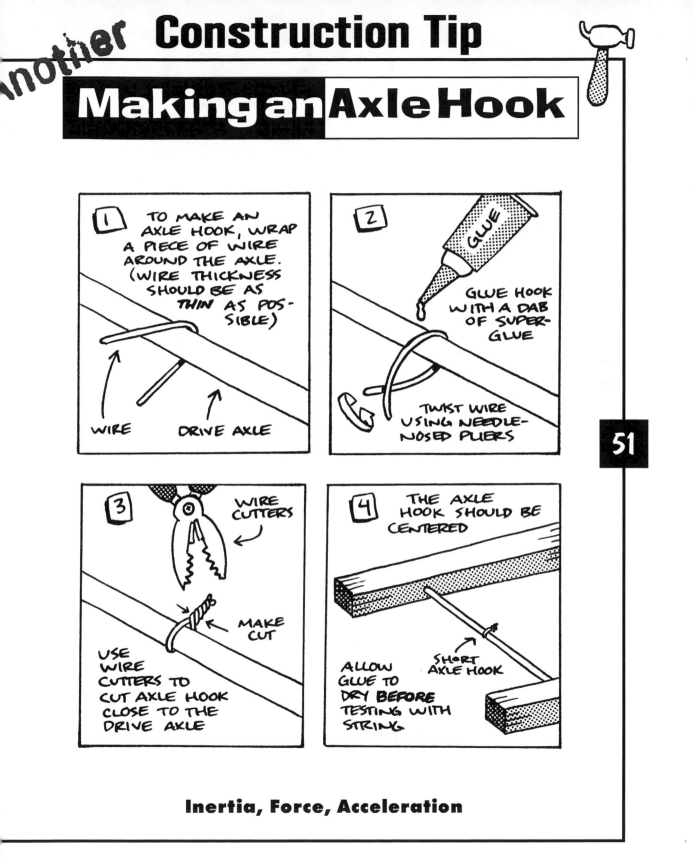

1 TO MAKE AN AXLE HOOK, WRAP A PIECE OF WIRE AROUND THE AXLE. (WIRE THICKNESS SHOULD BE AS *THIN* AS POSSIBLE)

WIRE

DRIVE AXLE

2 GLUE

GLUE HOOK WITH A DAB OF SUPER-GLUE

TWIST WIRE USING NEEDLE-NOSED PLIERS

3 WIRE CUTTERS

MAKE CUT

USE WIRE CUTTERS TO CUT AXLE HOOK CLOSE TO THE DRIVE AXLE

4 THE AXLE HOOK SHOULD BE CENTERED

SHORT AXLE HOOK

ALLOW GLUE TO DRY **BEFORE** TESTING WITH STRING

51

Inertia, Force, Acceleration

Momentum

With a distance car, you want to build the **lightest possible vehicle**, although heavy cars can perform well due to their momentum. That is, more massive cars, once moving, will have a greater resistance to change in their motion when compared to lighter cars. Massive vehicles will tend to maintain their motion, coasting farther than a lighter vehicle (given the same force of friction acting against the vehicle). This is because massive cars can take advantage of what is called **momentum**, which means **inertia in motion**. This sounds like a good idea for building a distance car, but there is a down side to this idea. You have to first get this more massive car moving in order to take advantage of its momentum. Heavy cars will be harder to start because of their inertia, so the pulling force will be larger using more energy at the start to accelerate. In order to increase the **pulling force** you will have to use a shorter lever arm on your mouse trap. This usually means that the car will not be pulled as far as slower vehicles with longer lever arms. With momentum you are counting on coasting distance, not pulling distance.

The down side is that heavier vehicles will have to travel faster and will therefore experience greater air resistance. This consumes more energy and ultimately the vehicle will not travel as far as a slow moving, energy-conserving vehicle.

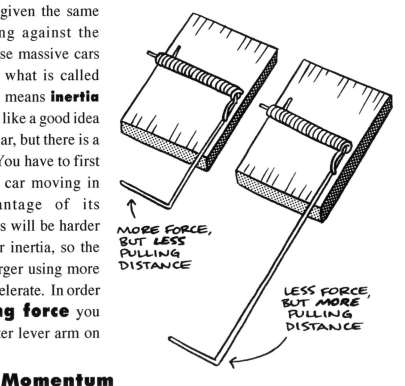

MORE FORCE, BUT LESS PULLING DISTANCE

LESS FORCE, BUT MORE PULLING DISTANCE

52

Momentum

Chassis Construction

One obvious consideration in the construction of your mouse-trap car is the **frame** or the **chassis**. The chassis is a mechanical component that must provide structural support for the motor, wheels, axles, etc. It is important that your mouse-trap car's chassis is designed to handle the operations of your vehicle. There are some important trade-offs that need to be considered. A chassis that is too light may be too delicate to handle the force of a wound up mouse-trap spring. Also, a chassis that is too light will have less weight pushing down on the wheels, causing less tire traction. A chassis that is too heavy will require more energy at the start than a lighter frame. The chassis needs to be **strong** and **stiff**. Strong means that it will not beak under a load. Stiff means it will not bend or has little flex. The first step to a strong, stiff, and light chassis is choosing the right materials. Balsa wood, pine, or bass wood are excellent choices although balsa wood is somewhat brittle and hard to drill holes into without ripping. Other materials can also be used for making a light weight strong and stiff frame. These include **Styrofoam®**, corrugated cardboard, plastics, aluminum and brass tubing.

Strength

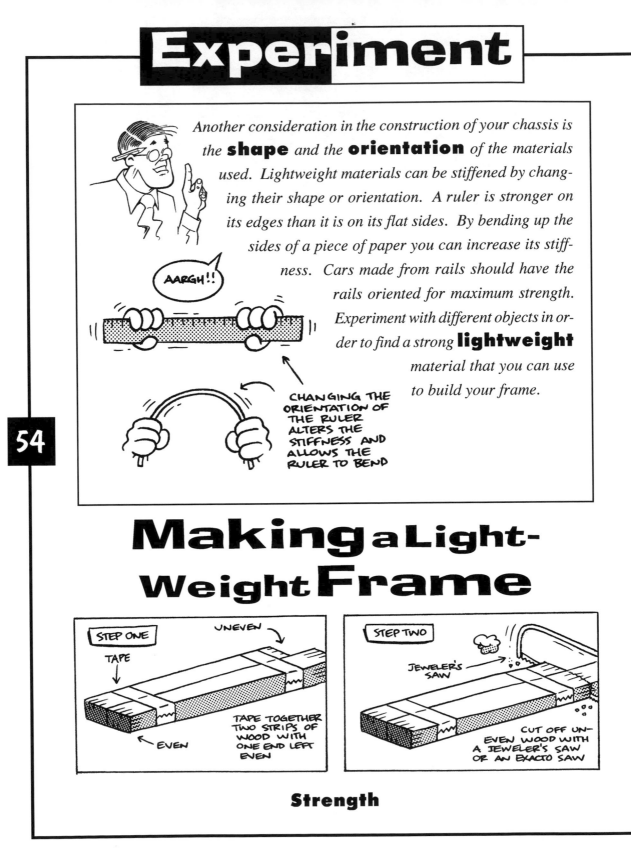

Another consideration in the construction of your chassis is the **shape** and the **orientation** of the materials used. Lightweight materials can be stiffened by changing their shape or orientation. A ruler is stronger on its edges than it is on its flat sides. By bending up the sides of a piece of paper you can increase its stiffness. Cars made from rails should have the rails oriented for maximum strength. Experiment with different objects in order to find a strong **lightweight** material that you can use to build your frame.

AARGH!!

54

CHANGING THE ORIENTATION OF THE RULER ALTERS THE STIFFNESS AND ALLOWS THE RULER TO BEND

Making a Light-Weight Frame

STEP ONE

UNEVEN

TAPE

EVEN

TAPE TOGETHER TWO STRIPS OF WOOD WITH ONE END LEFT EVEN

STEP TWO

JEWELER'S SAW

CUT OFF UN-EVEN WOOD WITH A JEWELER'S SAW OR AN EXACTO SAW

Strength

Construction Tip

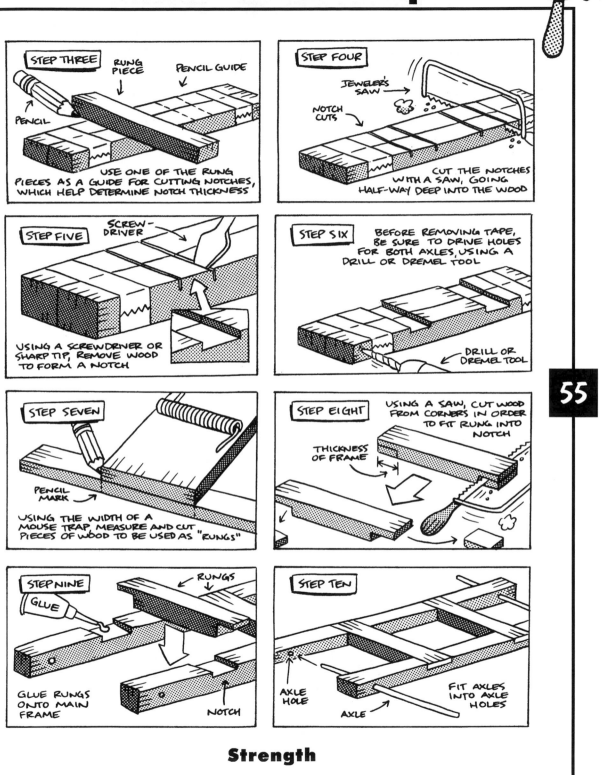

STEP THREE

PENCIL · RUNG PIECE · PENCIL GUIDE

USE ONE OF THE RUNG PIECES AS A GUIDE FOR CUTTING NOTCHES, WHICH HELP DETERMINE NOTCH THICKNESS

STEP FOUR

JEWELER'S SAW · NOTCH CUTS

CUT THE NOTCHES WITH A SAW, GOING HALF-WAY DEEP INTO THE WOOD

STEP FIVE

SCREW-DRIVER

USING A SCREWDRIVER OR SHARP TIP, REMOVE WOOD TO FORM A NOTCH

STEP SIX

BEFORE REMOVING TAPE, BE SURE TO DRIVE HOLES FOR BOTH AXLES, USING A DRILL OR DREMEL TOOL

DRILL OR DREMEL TOOL

STEP SEVEN

PENCIL MARK

USING THE WIDTH OF A MOUSE TRAP, MEASURE AND CUT PIECES OF WOOD TO BE USED AS "RUNGS"

STEP EIGHT

USING A SAW, CUT WOOD FROM CORNERS IN ORDER TO FIT RUNG INTO NOTCH

THICKNESS OF FRAME

STEP NINE

GLUE · RUNGS

GLUE RUNGS ONTO MAIN FRAME

NOTCH

STEP TEN

AXLE HOLE · AXLE

FIT AXLES INTO AXLE HOLES

Strength

Making a light-weight STRONG Lever Arm

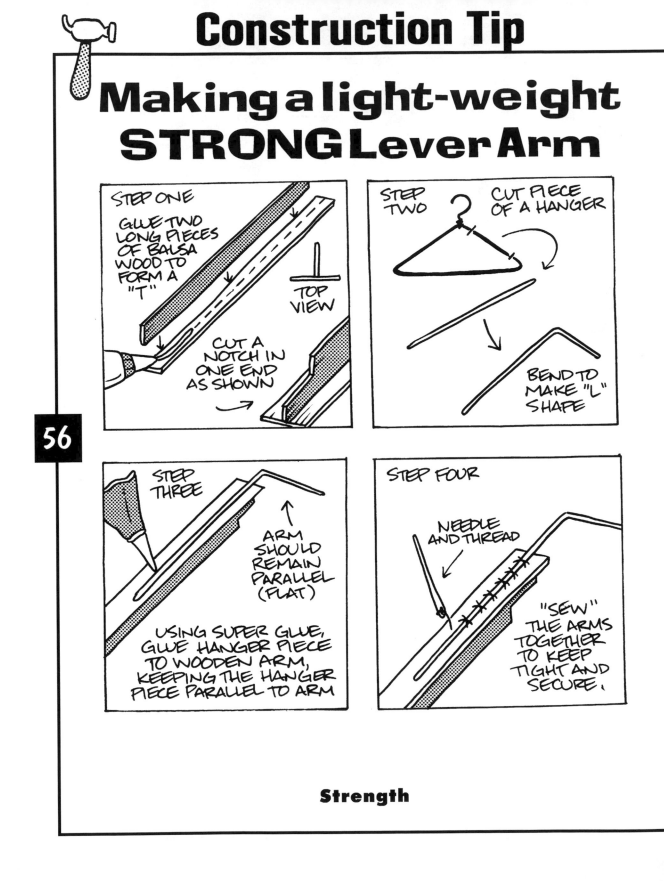

STEP ONE
GLUE TWO LONG PIECES OF BALSA WOOD TO FORM A "T"

TOP VIEW

CUT A NOTCH IN ONE END AS SHOWN →

STEP TWO
CUT PIECE OF A HANGER

BEND TO MAKE "L" SHAPE

STEP THREE
ARM SHOULD REMAIN PARALLEL (FLAT)

USING SUPER GLUE, GLUE HANGER PIECE TO WOODEN ARM, KEEPING THE HANGER PIECE PARALLEL TO ARM

STEP FOUR
NEEDLE AND THREAD

"SEW" THE ARMS TOGETHER TO KEEP TIGHT AND SECURE.

Strength

56

Construction Tip

A long lever arm will have a tendency to bend. This bending will prevent the spring from being fully **compressed** *or* **wound-up***. You can try using a brass brazing rod or steel rod for a real long lever arm but a better solution is making a light weight lever arm from balsa wood. This wooded lever arm will be* **stronger** *and* **lighter** *than any brass or steel rod that you could use and it will be much lighter. The strength of the wooden arm comes from its construction; two lightweight strips of balsa wood glued together to form 1/2 of an* **I-beam** *or a* **T-beam***. An I-beam or T-beam is much lighter and in some cases stronger than a solid piece of wood or steel.*

57

LIGHT WOODEN LEVER ARM

ARM SHOULD REACH REAR (DRIVE) AXLE

NOTCH ALLOWS LEVER ARM TO SIT FLAT AGAINST TRAP

35

Strength

Center of Mass

Center of mass is simply the average position of all particles of mass that make up an object. For symmetric objects of uniform density, such as a ball or a book, this point is usually at the geometrical center. But an irregularly shaped object, such as a baseball bat, will have more mass at one end, causing the center of mass to be located closer to the larger end. If a ball is thrown through the air, it will follow a smooth trajectory. In contrast, if a baseball bat is thrown through the air, it will seem

CENTER OF MASS

> As long as the **center of mass** is located above a point of support, an object will balance.

to **wobble** all over the place. The bat is actually wobbling around a single point—its center of mass—and that center of mass will follow a smooth trajectory. Objects that are rotating freely tend to rotate so that their center of mass travels smoothly (i.e., most energy efficient) with as little motion as possible. Objects that are forced to rotate around points that are not the center of mass consume more energy.

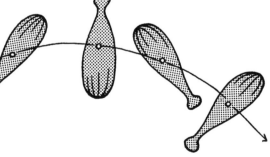

Larger wheels are affected more adversely by an offset center of mass than are smaller wheels. If the center of mass of a large wheel is not in the center of the wheel or through the axle, then the car will tend to wobble through its journey, wasting energy and decreasing the overall distance the car will travel. Also, it is

Center of Mass

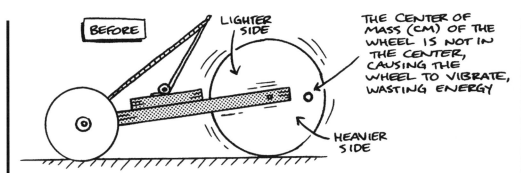

BEFORE

LIGHTER SIDE

THE CENTER OF MASS (CM) OF THE WHEEL IS NOT IN THE CENTER, CAUSING THE WHEEL TO VIBRATE, WASTING ENERGY

HEAVIER SIDE

possible for a car to **lose distance after stopping and begin rolling backward**; this occurs when the center of mass for a large wheel becomes located in an unstable position. As the center of mass begins to fall towards a more stable position, the wheel begins to rotate, causing the car to move either backward or forward. If the car moves forward, it will gain additional distance after stopping, but there is no way to predict where the center of mass will come to rest when the car stops. For this reason, it is best to **balance** a large wheel, forcing the center of mass to be located through the axle.

Large wheels should be balanced, especially if you have removed material from portions of the wheel in an effort to lighten the car. To balance a wheel, you should hold the wheel by the axle and allow it to turn freely. The heavier side of the wheel will fall towards the bottom. Once the heavier side is marked, mass can be added to the opposite side until the wheel has no tendency to rotate when suspended freely by the axle. Any material can be used to add mass to a large wheel, but **clay** and **pennies** are easy to work with.

59

AFTER

CM IS NOW IN THE CENTER, ALLOWING THE CAR TO ROLL SMOOTHLY, CONSERVING ENERGY

A PIECE OF CLAY IS USED AS A BALANCE TO PULL CM TOWARD THE CENTER OF ROTATION

Center of Mass

Experiment

Finding the Center of Mass

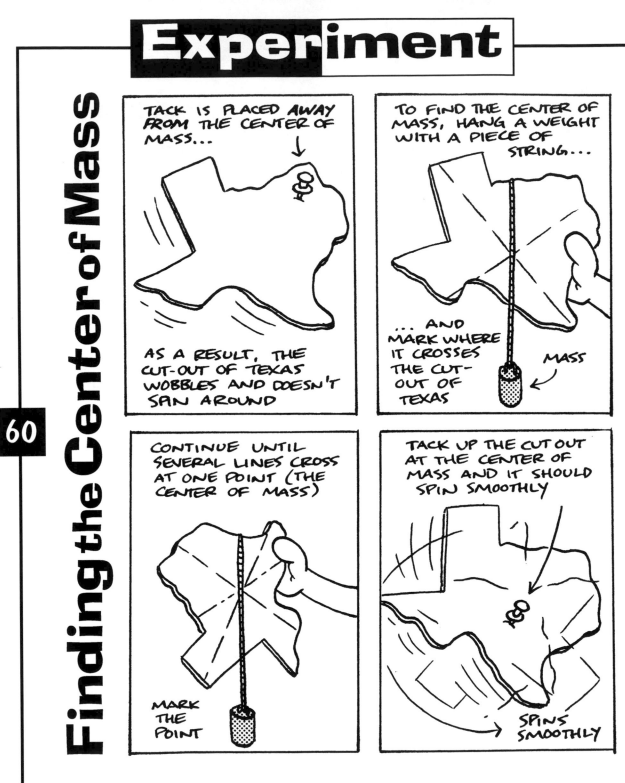

TACK IS PLACED *AWAY* FROM THE CENTER OF MASS...

AS A RESULT, THE CUT-OUT OF TEXAS WOBBLES AND DOESN'T SPIN AROUND

TO FIND THE CENTER OF MASS, HANG A WEIGHT WITH A PIECE OF STRING...

... AND MARK WHERE IT CROSSES THE CUT-OUT OF TEXAS

MASS

CONTINUE UNTIL SEVERAL LINES CROSS AT ONE POINT (THE CENTER OF MASS)

MARK THE POINT

TACK UP THE CUT OUT AT THE CENTER OF MASS AND IT SHOULD SPIN SMOOTHLY

SPINS SMOOTHLY

Center of Mass

Weight Distribution

Slippage of the drive wheels during the start **wastes energy**. There are several reasons for the slippage problem: not enough traction, too much pulling force or torque, and poor weight distribution. Traction is the grip your wheels have on the floor. You can increase the traction by adding a non-slipping material like a rubber band or Traction Action®, a sticky gel that is smeared on the wheels. If you try adding rubber bands and your car continues to slip on the start, then there are two other components which may be the cause of the problem: **torque** and/or **weight distribution**.

RUBBER BAND

If the mouse trap is placed too close to the pulling axle, the wheels will spin on the start. This problem is easy to correct by simply moving the trap away from the pulling axle and extending the lever arm.

61

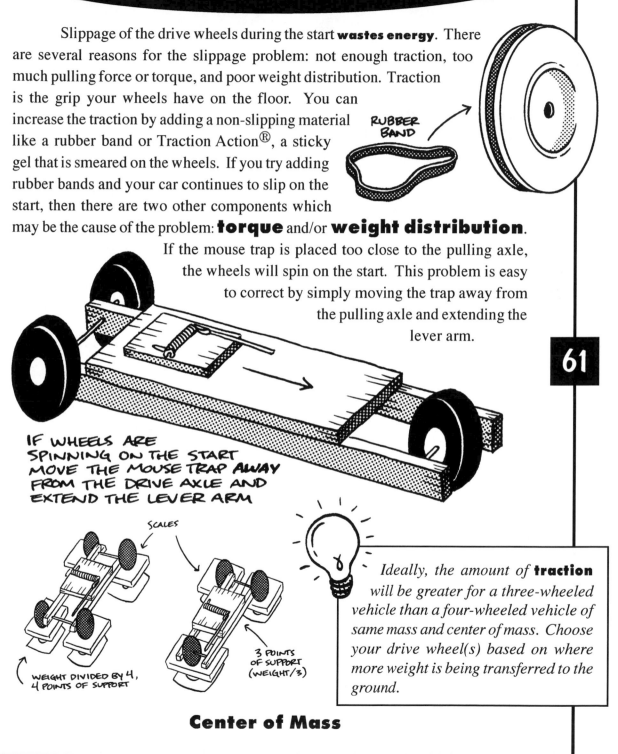

IF WHEELS ARE
SPINNING ON THE START
MOVE THE MOUSE TRAP AWAY
FROM THE DRIVE AXLE AND
EXTEND THE LEVER ARM

SCALES

WEIGHT DIVIDED BY 4,
4 POINTS OF SUPPORT

3 POINTS
OF SUPPORT
(WEIGHT/3)

Ideally, the amount of **traction** *will be greater for a three-wheeled vehicle than a four-wheeled vehicle of same mass and center of mass. Choose your drive wheel(s) based on where more weight is being transferred to the ground.*

Center of Mass

If the pulling wheels do not have enough traction, the problem may be because of the **distribution of the weight** of the car. Have you ever heard that front-wheel drive cars are better in snow and ice than rear-wheel drive vehicles? Front-wheel drive cars have the engine located directly above the drive wheels; this helps increase the traction on the front wheels. The closer the center of mass is located to the drive wheels, the more traction that will result. The balance point of your car, which represents the center of mass, should be located as close as possible to the drive wheels. If your car continues to slip on the start, you may want to try **adding some mass over or near the drive wheels** in order to shift the center of mass towards the drive train.

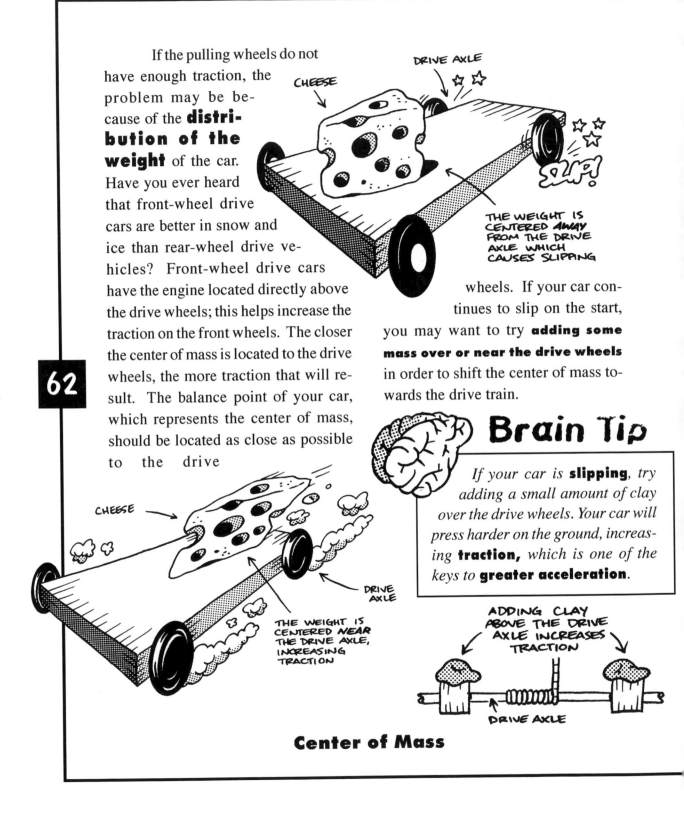

DRIVE AXLE

CHEESE

THE WEIGHT IS CENTERED *AWAY* FROM THE DRIVE AXLE WHICH CAUSES SLIPPING

SLIP!

CHEESE

DRIVE AXLE

THE WEIGHT IS CENTERED *NEAR* THE DRIVE AXLE, INCREASING TRACTION

62

Brain Tip

*If your car is **slipping**, try adding a small amount of clay over the drive wheels. Your car will press harder on the ground, increasing **traction**, which is one of the keys to **greater acceleration**.*

ADDING CLAY ABOVE THE DRIVE AXLE INCREASES TRACTION

DRIVE AXLE

Center of Mass

Rotational Inertia

Just as an object at rest tends to stay at rest and an object in motion tends to stay in motion, **an object rotating about an axis tends to remain rotating about the same axis unless an external force or torque acts on it**. The property of an object to resist changes in its rotational state of motion is called **rotational inertia** and is a restatement of Newton's First Law of Motion. **Rotational inertia is the resistance an object has to changes in rotation.** Just as inertia for linear motion depends on the mass of an object, so does rotational inertia. But rotational inertia also depends on one more element— the **location** of the mass with respect to the axis of rotation. The greater the distance between the bulk of an object's mass and its axis of rotation, the greater the rotational inertia. This principle is employed by a weightlifter when he or she twists a barbell with mass located on the ends. When the mass of the barbell is far from the axis of rotation, (i.e., its midpoint), the bar has considerable rotational inertia and is hard to turn or twist. If the mass is placed closer to the center of rotation, the bar twists with less effort. It follows that the greater the rotational inertia of an object, the harder it is to change the rotational state of that object. If rotating, it is difficult to stop; if at rest, it is difficult to rotate.

Experiment

Try an experiment to learn about **rotational inertia**. *Try twisting a barbell with the weight spaced close together and then far apart. You will definitely get a good feel for rotational inertia after this experiment.*

Rotational Inertia

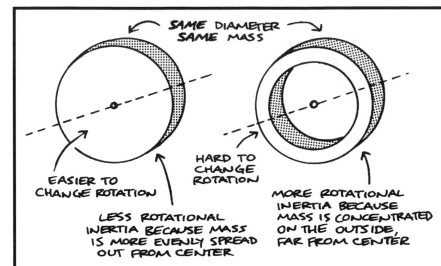

SAME DIAMETER
SAME MASS

EASIER TO
CHANGE ROTATION

HARD TO
CHANGE
ROTATION

LESS ROTATIONAL
INERTIA BECAUSE MASS
IS MORE EVENLY SPREAD
OUT FROM CENTER

MORE ROTATIONAL
INERTIA BECAUSE
MASS IS CONCENTRATED
ON THE OUTSIDE,
FAR FROM CENTER

Whether you are building a mouse-trap car for speed or distance, it is best to use wheels that have **as little rotational inertia as possible**. The less rotational inertia of your wheels, the less force that is needed to turn or accelerate your wheels. Especially with distance cars, you want to have the smallest possible pulling force. Smaller pulling forces will allow for greater pulling distances. Therefore, **less rotational inertia in the wheels means less required pulling force and greater travel distance** with higher acceleration off the start. Wheels with a large amount of rotational inertia will have a greater coasting distance, but this performance will be offset by the increased amounts of force and energy required to accelerate the vehicle off

the start. **Always pick wheels that are light weight.** Removing mass from the inside of your wheels using a Dremal tool or a drill will increase both speed and distance performance. This idea is extremely helpful in an effort to get cars to go faster off the start line or to get them to travel farther using less torque. Store-bought wheels are not always the best solution when determining the wheels for your vehicle. Some of the best wheels are found in your home: old compact discs, Styrofoam®, can lids and tops, records, mat board, or other lightweight materials. For distance vehicles, it is best to make your own wheels from light weight matte board. **In all cases, remove mass to form spoked wheels.**

COMPACT
DISK

DREM
TOO

Rotational Inertia

Construction Tip

Making a Wheel from a Compact Disc

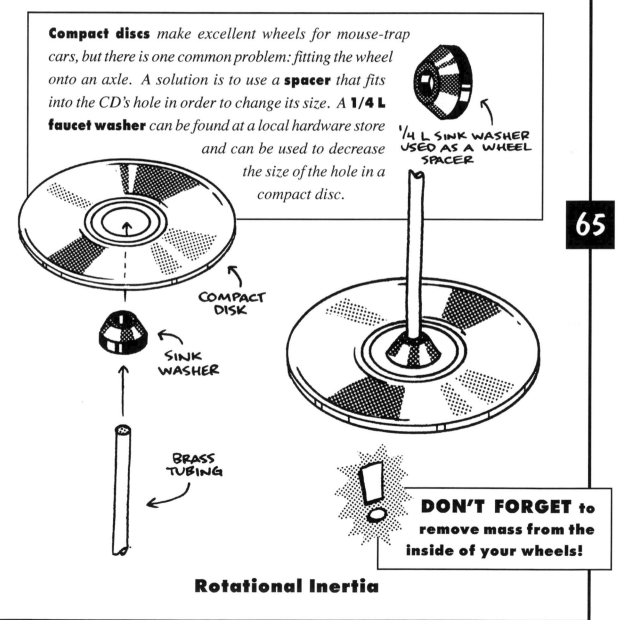

Compact discs *make excellent wheels for mouse-trap cars, but there is one common problem: fitting the wheel onto an axle. A solution is to use a* **spacer** *that fits into the CD's hole in order to change its size. A* **1/4 L faucet washer** *can be found at a local hardware store and can be used to decrease the size of the hole in a compact disc.*

1/4 L SINK WASHER USED AS A WHEEL SPACER

COMPACT DISK

SINK WASHER

BRASS TUBING

65

DON'T FORGET to remove mass from the inside of your wheels!

Rotational Inertia

Lab #4 - As The Wheels Turn

Purpose

In this activity you will find the rotational inertia of your wheels.

Materials

A Small Mass (no larger than 50g)
Stopwatch
String
Meter Stick
Pulley Set-up

Discussion

Rotational inertia is the resistance an object has to changing its state of rotation. The more rotational inertia a wheel has, the more torque that will be required to change its state of rotation. The torque is generated from the mousetrap's lever arm. More torque means shorter lever arms which translates into less pulling distance. With distance cars you want the longest possible pulling distance; therefore, you want a long lever arms. In most cases, whether you are building a speed or distance car it is best to have wheels with as little rotational inertia as possible. The less rotational inertia that a wheel has, the easier it will be to

Just as an object at rest tends to stay at rest and an object in motion tends to stay in motion, an object in a state of rotation about an axis tends to remain in that state of rotation about the same axis unless an external force or torque acts on it. Try an experiment to learn about rotational inertia. Try twisting a barbell with the weight spaced close together and then far apart. You will definitely get a good feel for rotational inertia after this experiment.

Rotational Inertia

The Set-up

accelerate the wheel and get the car moving. Rotational inertia is equal to the amount of torque acting on a system divided be the angular acceleration (Formula #1). The angular acceleration is equal to the linear acceleration divided by the radius of the wheel (Formula #2). The torque is equal to the applied force times the radius from the point of rotation (Formula #3). Putting Formula #1, #2 and #3 together you get Formula #4.

In this lab a weight is tied to a string and then wrapped around the axle of each wheel. The weight is allowed to fall causing the wheel(s) to spin. As the weight falls it is also timed. Based on the time it takes the weight to reach the tabletop or floor, you can calculate the rotational resistance of your wheel(s). The weight, as it falls, is being pulled downwards by gravity and upwards by the resistance of the wheel(s). The greater the rotational resistance or inertia, the longer it will take the weight to fall. The acceleration of the falling weight is found by Formula #5. Combine Formula #4 and #5 to get one formula that will be used for this lab to calculate the rotational inertia, based on the time of fall for the hanging mass. The total rotational inertia is the combination of all wheels added together.

Rotational Inertia

In this lab a weight is tied to a string and then wound around an axle. Based on the time it takes the weight to reach the tabletop or floor, you can calculate the rotational resistance of your wheel(s). The greater the rotational resistance or inertia, the longer it will take the weight to fall.

I = Rotational Inertia
τ = Torque
α = Angular Acceleration
a = Linear Acceleration
F = Applied Force
r = Lever Length
h = Fall Height of Mass
v_0 = Starting Falling Velocity (zero in this lab)
t = Time of Fall for Mass
a = Linear Acceleration

68

Formulas

Formula #1: $\tau = Fr$

Formula #2: $I = \dfrac{\tau}{\alpha}$

Formula #3: $\alpha = \dfrac{a}{r}$

Angular acceleration based on linear acceleration

Formula #4: $I = \dfrac{Fr}{\dfrac{a}{r}}$

Formulas 1 - 3 combined

Formula #5: $I = \dfrac{Fr^2}{a}$

Rotational inertia from Formula #3 based on linear acceleration

Formula #6: $h = v_0 t + \dfrac{1}{2}at^2$

The height of fall based on an accelerating object through time

Formula #7: $a = \dfrac{2h}{t^2}$

Solving for acceleration

Rotational Inertia

Formula #8: $I = \dfrac{Fr^2\,t^2}{2h}$

Rotational inertia of a wheel based on a falling mass

Another Way to Get The Job Done

If your wheel(s) is (are) not glued to the axle, then you may have to design a test device to hold and measure the rotational inertia. Design a pulley apparatus that can hold each of your wheels and that will allow them to spin freely. The smaller the pulley or axle that the string is wrapped around, the smaller the acceleration of the falling mass, which makes timing more accurate.

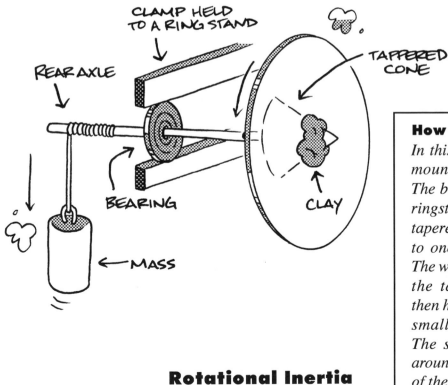

CLAMP HELD
TO A RING STAND

REAR AXLE

TAPPERED CONE

BEARING

CLAY

MASS

Rotational Inertia

How it Works:

In this set-up an axle is mounted in a bearing. The bearing is held to a ringstand by a clamp. A tapered cone is attached to one end of the axle. The wheel is placed onto the tapered cone and then held in place with a small amount of clay. The string is wrapped around the opposite side of the axle.

Let's Get Spinning

IMPORTANT: Steps 1-5 are only for those who test their wheels on a pulley system. If you art measuring your wheels' rotational inertia on your vehicle's axles, then skip to Step 6.

Finding the rotational inertia of the pulley set-up

Step 1: Because the pulley set-up has rotational inertia of its own you will have to calculate its rotational inertia in order to subtract it from that of your wheel. Make the following data table:

Data Table #1

Fall Distance of Mass	Time of Fall	Radius of Pulley	Weight of Falling Mass	Rotational Inertia of Pulley
$d_1=$	$t_1=$	$r_p=$	$W=$	$I_{pulley\ 1}=$
$d_2=$	$t_2=$	$r_p=$	$W=$	$I_{pulley\ 2}=$
$d_3=$	$t_3=$	$r_p=$	$W=$	$I_{pulley\ 3}=$
$d_4=$	$t_4=$	$r_p=$	$W=$	$I_{pulley\ 4}=$
AVE	$t=$		$W=$	$I_{pulley}=$

Step 2: Calculate the weight of your hanging mass by dividing grams by 1000 and then multiplying by 9.8. This will give you weight in Newtons. Record in the data table as W. It is best to use a smaller mass no larger than 50g. I suggest 20g. Attach the weight to the end of a string that is long enough to reach from the pulley to the floor or table top, depending on the fall distance that you will use for your measurement. Attach the other end of the string to the axle or pulley set-up and wind the string up around your setup.

Step 3: Measure the fall distance from the bottom of the hanging weight to the surface below and record this measurement as fall distance of mass (d). Measure the radius of the axle or pulley where the string is wound and record as the pulley radius (r).

Rotational Inertia

Step 4: Allow the weight to fall while timing with a stopwatch and record the time in the data table (t). Repeat several times and record in the Data Table #1. Find an average. Make sure that you drop the weight from the same point each time that you repeat the experiment.

Step 5: Using the following formula, calculate the rotational inertia of your pulley.

$$I = \frac{Fr^2 \, t^2}{2h}$$

$$I_{\text{Rotational Inertia of pulley}} = \frac{(\text{Weight of Hanging Mass}) * (\text{Radius of Pully})^2 * (\text{Time of Fall})^2}{2 * (\text{Distance that mass falls})}$$

Finding the rotational inertia of your wheels

Step 6: Depending on whether you will measure each wheel by itself or if you will measure the rotational inertia of an axle system, make a copy of Data Table #2 for each wheel or axle system for your vehicle. If you had to perform steps 1-5 then record the average rotational inertia from your pulley set-up in Data Table #2.

Data Table #2   (Front Axle System or Wheel #1)

Fall Distance of Mass	Time of Fall	Radius of Pulley	Weight of Falling Mass	Rotational Inertia of Pulley	Rotational Inertia of Wheel
$d_1=$	$t_1=$	$r_p=$	$W=$	$I_{pulley}=$	$I_{wheel\,1}=$
$d_2=$	$t_2=$	$r_p=$	$W=$	$I_{pulley}=$	$I_{wheel\,2}=$
$d_3=$	$t_3=$	$r_p=$	$W=$	$I_{pulley}=$	$I_{wheel\,3}=$
$d_4=$	$t_4=$	$r_p=$	$W=$	$I_{pulley}=$	$I_{wheel\,4}=$
AVE	$t=$				$I_{wheel}=$

Rotational Inertia

Step 7: Attach one wheel at a time to the pulley apparatus if you are measuring each wheel by itself. If you are measuring a complete axle system, then perform the following:

Attach one end of a string to the axle and the other end of a weight. The string should be long enough to reach the surface below. Calculate the weight of your hanging mass by dividing grams by 1000 and then multiplying by 9.8. This will give you weight in Newtons. Record in the data table as W. It is best to use a smaller mass no larger than 50g. I suggest 20g. Wind the string around the axle and measure the starting position of the mass so that in all trials the mass falls from the same height.

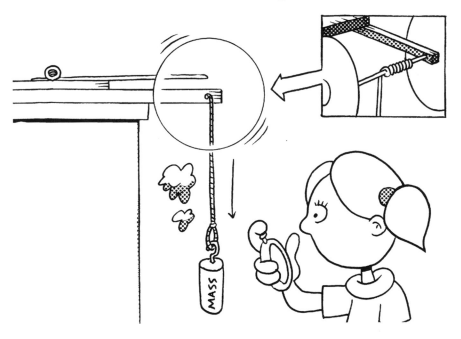

Step 8: Allow the weight to fall while timing with a stopwatch and record the time in the data table (t). Repeat several times and record in the Data Table #2. Find an average. Make sure that you drop the weight from the same point each time that you repeat the experiment.

Rotational Inertia

Step 9:
Using the following formula, calculate the rotational inertia of your wheel. Look carefully at the formula. It is the same as in Step 5 except this time you have to remove the rotational inertial of the pulley. Do not forget to subtract the resistance inertia of the pulley! If you did not use a pulley set-up ignore the rotatioanl inertia of the pulley and plug in all variables except for the rotational inertia of the pulley.

Rotational Inertia of a Wheel or an Axle System

$$I_{\text{Rotational Inertia of Wheel}} = \frac{(\text{Weight of Hanging Mass}) * (\text{Radius of Pully})^2 * (\text{Time of Fall})^2}{2 * (\text{Distance that mass falls})} - I_{\text{Pulley}}$$

Step 10:
Repeat for each wheel or axle system of your car and record your results in Data Table #3 as follows: "Front Wheel #1," "Rear Wheel #2," or "Front Axle system," "Rear Axle system" .

Data Table #3

	Front Wheel #1 Or Front Axle System	Front Wheel #2	Rear Wheel #1 Or Rear Axle System	Rear Wheel #2
Rotational Inertia	$I_{f1}=$	$I_{f2}=$	$I_{r1}=$	$I_{r2}=$
Radius of Wheel	$r_{f1}=$	$r_{f2}=$	$r_{r1}=$	$r_{r2}=$

Step 11:
Add the rotational inertia for all components together in order to get the total rotational inertia.

Total Rotational Inertia = _____ kg • m^2

Rotational Inertia

Energy

Perhaps the concept most central to building mouse-trap cars is **energy**. Energy is defined as having the ability to do work. Work is motion that result in something being done. Without energy, the universe would be motionless and without life. We usually observe energy only when it is happening or when it is being transformed. Energy can be classified in a number of ways. Most commonly energy is classified as **potential** and **kinetic**. The energy that is stored and held in readiness is called potential energy (PE) because in the stored state it has the potential to do work. For example, a stretched or compressed spring has the potential for doing work. When a bow is drawn, energy is stored in the bow. A stretched rubber band has potential energy because of its position and because in this position it is capable of doing work. Kinetic energy (KE) is energy of motion or the energy a moving object has. A baseball thrown through the air has kinetic energy because of its motion just as a moving car has energy because of its speed or motion.

Energy, potential or kinetic, follows one basic rule called the Law of Conservation of Energy, stated: **Energy cannot be created or destroyed; it may be transformed from one form into another, but the total amount of energy never changes.** By winding the spring on your mouse-trap car, you store energy in the spring as potential energy. This stored potential energy will turn into kinetic energy as the mouse-trap car begins to move. In a perfect universe, your mouse-trap car should roll

POTENTIAL ENERGY (PE)

KINETIC ENERGY (KE)

74

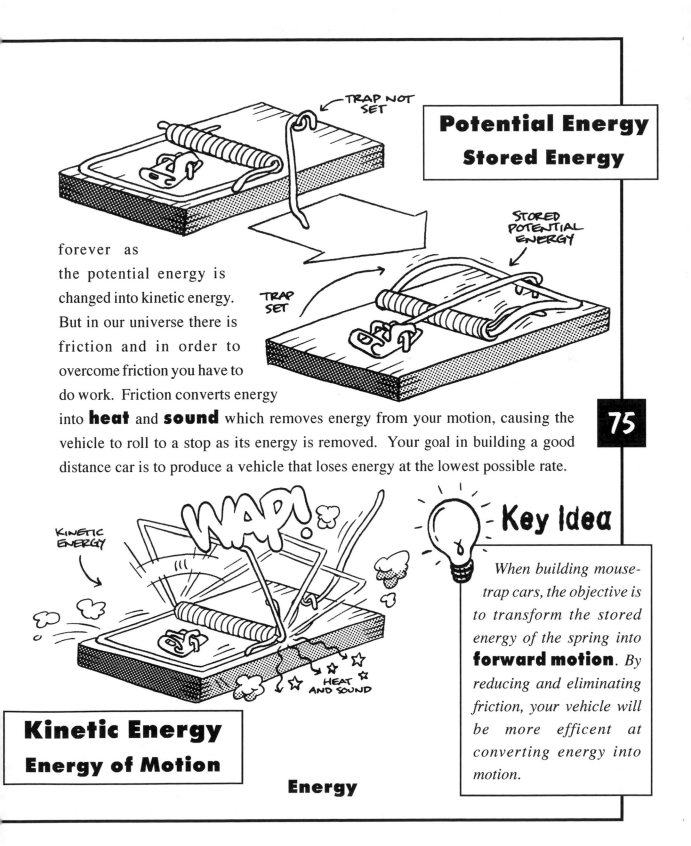

Potential Energy
Stored Energy

TRAP NOT SET

STORED POTENTIAL ENERGY

TRAP SET

forever as the potential energy is changed into kinetic energy. But in our universe there is friction and in order to overcome friction you have to do work. Friction converts energy into **heat** and **sound** which removes energy from your motion, causing the vehicle to roll to a stop as its energy is removed. Your goal in building a good distance car is to produce a vehicle that loses energy at the lowest possible rate.

WAP!

KINETIC ENERGY

HEAT AND SOUND

Kinetic Energy
Energy of Motion

Energy

-**Key Idea**

When building mouse-trap cars, the objective is to transform the stored energy of the spring into **forward motion**. *By reducing and eliminating friction, your vehicle will be more effecient at converting energy into motion.*

Lab #5- All Wound Up

Purpose

To calculate the starting potential energy and to find the spring coefficient.

Equipment Needed

Spring Scale or a Computer Force Probe
Tension Wheel (recommended but not needed)
String

Discussion

Energy has the ability to do work. Your mousetrap car's performance will depend directly on the strength of your mousetrap's spring. The stored energy of your spring in the fully wound-up position is called potential energy. The amount of stored potential energy is the same as the work that was required to wind the spring. The force required to wind the spring times the distance the force was applied is equal to the work that was done on the spring (Formula #1). Because the force required to wind the spring changes and depends on how much the spring is wound, you will have to find the average force between a series of points and then calculate the work done between those marks. The total work (or the stored potential energy) is equal to all the changes of energy between all the points added together (Formula #2). In order to measure the winding force you have to use a spring scale attached to a lever. The lever is lifted and the force is measured every 5 or 10 degrees. The scale has to be held such that the string attached to the lever arm is perpendicular. A problem with this method is that as the spring scale is held in different positions it becomes inaccurate. The spring scale cannot change from the position at which it was zeroed. For this reason I recommend using a tension wheel. A tension wheel allows the spring scale to remain in one position, producing more accurate results and it is easier to use.

Potential Energy, Spring Constant

The Set-up

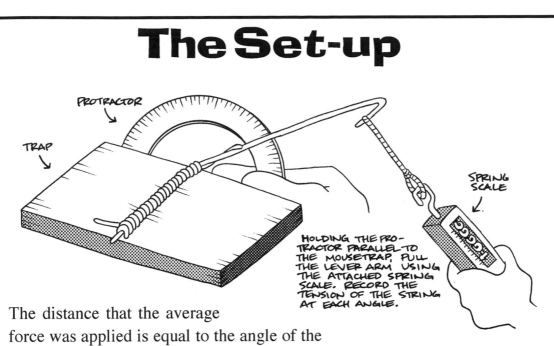

PROTRACTOR

TRAP

SPRING SCALE

HOLDING THE PRO-
TRACTOR PARALLEL TO
THE MOUSETRAP, PULL
THE LEVER ARM USING
THE ATTACHED SPRING
SCALE. RECORD THE
TENSION OF THE STRING
AT EACH ANGLE.

The distance that the average force was applied is equal to the angle of the measurement in radians times the length of the measuring lever arm. If you are using a tension wheel, then the radius of the wheel is the measuring lever arm (Formula #3). Formula #4 allows you to convert from degrees to radians.

For a spring that is stretched or compressed longitudinally, Hooke's Law applies and says that the force is equal to the spring constant times the stretching or compressing displacement. But a mousetrap spring does not stretch longitudinally. A mousetrap spring is a torsion spring and winds up. For this type of spring a different formula is needed (Formula #5). It is a torque that must be applied to the spring to wind it and the displacement is measured in radians (Formula #6). The units associated with the spring constant become Newtons * Meters/ Radians. For a spring that compresses or stretches in a linear direction, the total potential energy is one half the spring constant times the displacement squared (Formula #7). For a torsion spring the displacement is substituted by the angle in radians (Formula #8).

Potential Energy, Spring Constant

Tools of the Trade: Tension Wheel

A **tension wheel** is designed to direct the pulling force in the same direction as the spring is wound. This prevents the scale from having to be re-zeroed as its direction of pull changes. Degree markings make it easy to measure force and angle.

EACH DASH REPRESENTS A DEGREE, OR ANGLE. USING THIS TECHNIQUE, YOU CAN FIND THE TENSION OF YOUR STRING AT EACH ANGLE

SPRING SCALE

How it Works:

As the wheel is turned clockwise the spring on the mousetrap is compressed. The value of the spring constant depends on the material the spring is made from, the diameter of the wire, the diameter of the coil, and the number of coils.

Need A Tool?

This tool can be ordered from Doc Fizzix at (512) 218-0454
www.docfizzix.com

Formulas

What it All Means

W = Work
F = Force
d = Displacement
k = Linear Spring Constant
κ = Torsion Spring Constant
x = Spring Displacement
τ = Torque
θ = Angle
PE = Potential Energy

Formula #1: $W = F \cdot d$

Work formula used with a constant (non-changing) force

Formula #2: $W = \int_0^{\pi r} F_{(x)} \; d_{(x)}$

Work formula used with a changing force as
with a mousetrap spring

Formula #3: $d = \theta \, r$

A formula to calculate the linear distance of travel for a wheel

Formula #4: $\text{degrees} \times \dfrac{\pi}{180°} = \theta$

A formula used to change degrees into radians

79

Formula #5: $F = -kx$

Hooke's Law. Force of a stretched or compressed spring

Formula #6: $\tau = \kappa\theta$

From Hooke's Law. Used to calculate the torque from a torsional spring

Formula #7: $PE = \dfrac{1}{2} kx^2$

Potential energy of a stretched or compressed spring

Formula #8: $PE = \dfrac{1}{2} \kappa\theta^2$

Potential energy of a stretched or compressed torsion spring

Potential Energy, Spring Constant

Pulling Your Weight

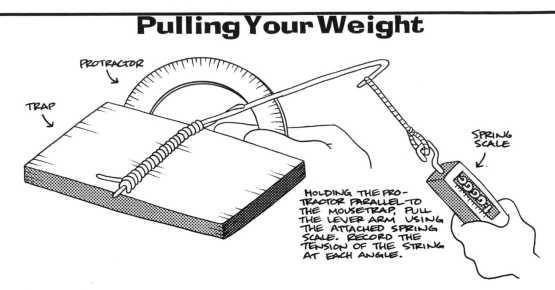

PROTRACTOR

TRAP

SPRING SCALE

HOLDING THE PRO-
TRACTOR PARALLEL TO
THE MOUSETRAP, PULL
THE LEVER ARM USING
THE ATTACHED SPRING
SCALE. RECORD THE
TENSION OF THE STRING
AT EACH ANGLE.

Step 1: In this lab you can use either a spring scale or a force probe in order to measure the spring's tension at different points along its travel. Start by attaching a string to the end of your mousetrap's extended lever arm. The point where you attach the string on the mousetrap's lever arm must extend pass the edge of the mousetrap's base so that all measurements can be taken from 0 to 180 degrees without the mousetrap's base blocking the measuring process. The string should be about 20 centimeters in length or less. Attach the spring scale to the other end of the string. Hold or attach a protractor to the mousetrap so that the center point of the protractor is in the middle of the spring and the zero degree point on the protractor is lined up with the starting point of the relaxed lever arm.

Step 2: Start at "0" degrees and pull up on the lever arm with the spring scale until the lever arm "just" lifts up from the base of the mousetrap and record this measurement as the starting force. Continue to pull up on the spring scale, stopping at every 5 or 10 degrees. Record the tension at each point in the data table. You must keep the scale perpendicular to the lever arm at each point you measure. Record the tension and angle in the data table.

Potential Energy, Spring Constant

Recommendations:
*Try to set-up a **spread sheet** on a computer in order to handle your data more **efficiently**.*

Data Tables

Data Table #1

Angle	Tension	Change in Radians	Total Radians	Change in Displacement	Total Displacement
5	$F_0 =$	$\Delta\theta_0 = 0$	$\theta_0 = 0$	$\Delta d_0 = 0$	$d_0 = 0$
10	$F_1 =$	$\Delta\theta_1 =$	$\theta_1 =$	$\Delta d_1 =$	$d_1 =$
15	$F_2 =$	$\Delta\theta_2 =$	$\theta_2 =$	$\Delta d_2 =$	$d_2 =$
20	$F_3 =$	$\Delta\theta_3 =$	$\theta_3 =$	$\Delta d_3 =$	$d_3 =$
25	$F_4 =$	$\Delta\theta_4 =$	$\theta_4 =$	$\Delta d_4 =$	$d_4 =$
180	$F_{36} =$	$\Delta\theta_{36} =$	$\theta_{36} =$	$\Delta d_{36} =$	$d_{36} =$

Data Table #2

Spring Constant	Torque	Change in Potential Energy	Total Potential Energy
$k_0 = 0$	$T_0 =$	$\Delta PE_0 = 0$	$PE_0 = 0$
$k_1 =$	$T_1 =$	$\Delta PE_1 =$	$PE_{0-1} =$
$k_2 =$	$T_2 =$	$\Delta PE_2 =$	$PE_{0-2} =$
$k_3 =$	$T_3 =$	$\Delta PE_3 =$	$PE_{0-3} =$
$k_4 =$	$T_4 =$	$\Delta PE_4 =$	$PE_{0-4} =$
$k_{36} =$	$T_{36} =$	$\Delta PE_{36} =$	$PE_{0-36} =$
Ave		Total	

Potential Energy, Spring Constant

Step 3: Calculate the change in radians for each angle and record them in the data table. If each measurement was made at the same increment (e.g., 5, 10, 15, 20 ...) you can use the same change in radians for all angles. Use the following method to calculate the change in radians:

$$\Delta\theta_1 = (\text{degrees}_1 - \text{degrees}_0) \times \frac{\pi}{180°}$$

$$\Delta\theta_2 = (\text{degrees}_2 - \text{degrees}_1) \times \frac{\pi}{180°}$$

Step 4: Measure the length of the lever arm from the spring to the point where the scale was attached to the arm and record this as the radius. Calculate the change in displacement, also known as the arc length, for each angle using the following formula. If each measurement was made at the same increment, (e.g. 5, 10, 15, 20 ...) you can use the same arc length (displacement) for all angles.

$$\Delta d_1 = \Delta\theta_1 r \qquad \Delta d_2 = \Delta\theta_2 r \qquad \Delta d_3 = \Delta\theta_3 r$$

Step 5: Calculate the total displacement for each angle by adding each of the previous changes in displacement to the next.

Step 6: Calculate the change in potential energy for each point using the following method. Multiply the average force between the starting and ending points with the change in distance. Add each of the change in PE values together in order to find the total potential energy from the column. This added value should be the energy your vehicle starts with before it is released.

Potential Energy, Spring Constant

$$\Delta PE_{0,1} = \frac{F_0 + F_1}{2} \cdot \Delta d_1$$

$$\Delta PE_{1,2} = \frac{F_1 + F_2}{2} \cdot \Delta d_2$$

$$\Delta PE_{2,3} = \frac{F_2 + F_3}{2} \cdot \Delta d_3$$

Step 7: Calculate the spring constant for each change in angle. The spring on a mousetrap is an example of a torsion spring, a spring that coils as opposed to one that stretches; use the following equation to calculate the spring constant: $\tau = \kappa\theta$. Torque is equal to the spring constant times the angle measured in radians. Torque is calculated from the force that is applied to a lever arm times the length of the lever arm $\tau = Fr_{\text{lever arm}}$. You will need to subtract the starting torque in order to find the actual change in torque for each change in angle. Total each spring constant and find an average.

$$\kappa = \frac{\tau}{\theta}$$

$$\kappa_1 = \frac{(F_1 - F_0)r_{\text{arm length}}}{\theta_{0,1}}$$

$$\kappa_2 = \frac{(F_2 - F_1)r_{\text{arm length}}}{\theta_{1,2}}$$

$$\kappa_3 = \frac{(F_3 - F_2)r_{\text{arm length}}}{\theta_{2,3}}$$

Potential Energy, Spring Constant

Graphing the results

In each of the following graphs attempt to draw the best fit lines. If data is widely scattered do not attempt to connect each dot but instead draw the best shape of the dots. If you have access to a computer, you can use a spread sheet like Microsoft Excel to plot your data.

1. Graph **Pulling Force** on the vertical axis and the **Displacement** on the horizontal axis.

2. Graph **Torque** on the vertical axis and **Angle in Radians** on the horizontal.

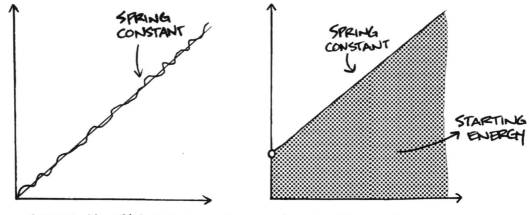

GRAPHING THE TENSION AT EACH ANGLE, YOU CAN GET THE **SPRING CONSTANT** AND THE **STARTING ENERGY**. YOUR RESULTS SHOULD ROUGHLY FORM A STRAIGHT LINE.

Potential Energy, Spring Constant

Analysis

1. The slope from your graph of "torque vs. angle" represents the spring constant. Does the slope change or remain constant? Do you have an ideal spring that follows Hooke's Law?

2. What does the slope of the line from each of your graphs tell you about the strength of your spring compared to other students' graphs?

3. Calculate the area under all parts of the best-fit line from the graph of "torque vs. angle." This number represents the potential energy you are starting with. The larger the number, the more energy you have to do work. This number should be close to the total potential energy calculated from your data table. How does the slope compare to the number in the data table?

4. How does your potential energy compare to other students' potential energy in your class? Discuss.

Potential Energy, Spring Constant

When designing a mouse-trap powered car, there are two variables that truly determine the overall performance: **friction** and **energy**. Friction is what slows and stops your vehicle; energy is what moves your vehicle. If your vehicle encounters too much friction, your energy supply will be consumed too quickly and your vehicle will not travel very far or accelerate very fast. Evaluate every moving component on your vehicle and decrease the amount of friction at each point. As a general rule of thumb, the more moving components that a machine has, the greater the force of friction will be and the greater the energy consumption will be. **Your ultimate goal when building a distance mouse-trap powered vehicle is to reduce friction to the lowest possible force.** The smaller the frictional force, the farther your supply of energy will propel your vehicle. With this idea in mind, slow-moving vehicles will have a smaller force of air resistance acting against them and will travel farther than faster-moving vehicles.

FRICT LEV

AIR FRICTION

BEARING FRICTION

AIR FRICTI

86

Energy

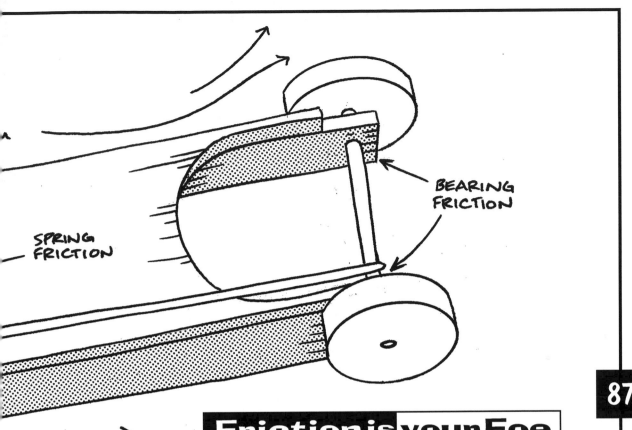

BEARING FRICTION

SPRING FRICTION

Friction is your Foe

It can not be said enough! *Your ultimate goal when building a distance mouse-trap powered vehicle is to reduce friction to the lowest possible force. The smaller the frictional force, the further your supply of energy will propel your vehicle or the faster your vehicle will travel. If you are building a distance car, your vehicle should move as slow as possible without stopping as the spring releases its energy. Look your car over with a scrutinizing eye in order to reduce the total amount of friction acting on your vehicle.*

Energy

Lab #6 - The force Against you, Part II

Purpose
To determine the force of friction against your vehicle.

Equipment Needed
Meter Tape

Variables Needed From Other Labs
Total Potential Energy from Lab #5

Discussion
Mousetrap cars convert their starting energy into work. Work is done to overcome the frictional forces acting against the vehicle. In most cases the largest amount of friction is the rolling friction caused by the bearings on the axles. The total work that your car will do is equal to the starting energy of your vehicle that you calculated in Lab #4. The predicted travel distance is equal to the starting energy divided by the force of rolling friction. You should observe (by comparing your results to other students' results) that the less rolling friction that there is, the greater the distance a vehicle should travel.

$$\text{Formula \#8:} \quad PE = f_{rf}\, d$$

Work is equal to the starting energy.

$$\text{Formula \#9:} \quad d = \frac{PE}{f_{rf}}$$

The maximum distance depends on the starting energy and the force of rolling friction

Rolling Friction, Work

Calculate the Friction from the Actual Travel Distance

Step 1: Wind-up and release your vehicle. Measure the total travel distance. Test your result several times, then calculate the average travel distance for your vehicle.

Data Table #2

Trial #	Actual Travel Distance	Starting Energy	Friction	Coefficient of Rolling Friction
1	$d_1 =$	PE=	$f_1 =$	$\mu_1 =$
2	$d_2 =$	PE=	$f_2 =$	$\mu_2 =$
3	$d_3 =$	PE=	$f_3 =$	$\mu_3 =$
4	$d_4 =$	PE=	$f_4 =$	$\mu_4 =$
AVE	$d =$		$f =$	$\mu =$

Step 2: Calculate the rolling friction from the actual travel distance using the following formula:

$$\text{Work} = \text{Force} \cdot \text{Distance}$$

$$f_1 = \frac{PE_1}{d_1}$$

Step 3: You are going to calculate the coefficient of friction from the following formula. Note: For mass, remove the wheels and use ONLY the mass of the frame. It is the frame that rests on the bearings and presses the bearings' surfaces together. Therefore, you must remove the wheels and "mass" only the frame.

$$\mu = \frac{f}{mg}$$

Rolling Friction, Work

Power Output

There is no difference in the amount of energy expended when you walk up a flight of stairs and when you run up a flight of stairs, but there is a difference in the amount of **power** output in the two situations. More power is expended running up the stairs. Power is the rate at which you do work or use energy. Because running up the stairs allows you to get to the top more quickly, you use energy at a higher rate. Higher power ratings mean that more work is being done per second when compared to smaller power ratings. A watt is the unit of measurement for power. A 120 watt light bulb uses twice the energy each second compared to a 60 watt light bulb. Usually higher rates of energy consumption will waste more energy to heat and sound than lower power outputs.

When you build a mouse-trap car for distance, you want a small energy consumption per second or a small power usage. **Smaller power outputs will produce less wasted energy and greater efficiency**. When you build a vehicle for speed, you want to use your energy quickly or at a high power ratio. You can change the power ratio of your vehicle by changing one or all of the following: where the string attaches to the mouse-trap's lever arm, the drive wheel diameter, or the drive axle diameter.

The amount of energy used by a short lever arm and a long lever arm are the same, but the distance that the energy is used determines that rate of energy consumption or the power. Long lever arms decrease the pulling force but increase the pulling distance, thereby decreasing the power. Short lever arms increase the pulling force and decrease the pulling distance, thereby increasing the power. **If you are building a mouse-trap car for speed, you will want the maximum power output** just before the point where the wheels begin to spin-out on the floor. Maximum power output means a higher rate of stored energy is being transferred into energy of motion or greater acceleration of the vehicle. Greater acceleration can be achieved by having a short length lever arm or by having a small axle to a large wheel. **If you are building a distance vehicle, you want to minimize the power output** or transfer stored energy into energy of motion at a slow rate. This usually mean having a long lever arm and a large axle-to-wheel ratio. If you make the lever arm too long, you may not have enough torque through the entire pulling distance to keep the vehicle moving, in which case you will have to attach the string to a lower point or change the axle-to-wheel ratio.

MORE POWER

LESS POWER

91

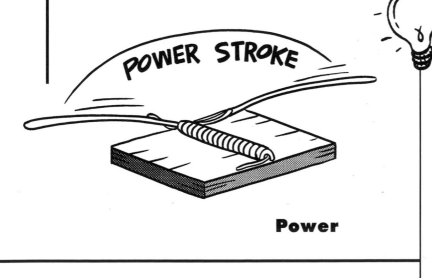

POWER STROKE

Power

When the string is wound around the axle, the spring of the trap is under maximum tension and has the most potential energy. As the mousetrap's arm is released, the mousetrap converts potential energy into kinetic energy. The **power stroke** *represents the range of the lever arms movement and the total available energy.*

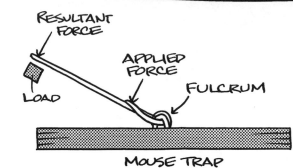

MOUSE TRAP

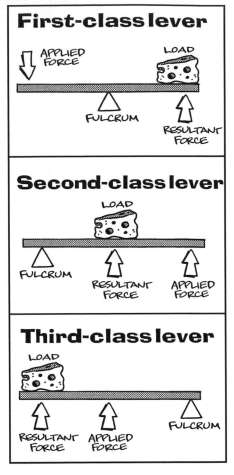

First-class lever

APPLIED FORCE — LOAD — FULCRUM — RESULTANT FORCE

Second-class lever

LOAD — FULCRUM — RESULTANT FORCE — APPLIED FORCE

Third-class lever

LOAD — RESULTANT FORCE — APPLIED FORCE — FULCRUM

A Mousetrap is a Third-class lever

92

Mechanical advantage **comparison between the force put into a machine and the force out of a machine.** Mechanical advantage calculated from the resultant force divided by the applied force. An example of a "simple" machine is a lever. With a lever you have four important elements that you must identify: the applied force, the resultant force, the fulcrum, and the load. The applied force is put into the machine and the resultant force is what comes out of the machine. The load is what the machine is doing the work on and the fulcrum is where a lever pivots or rotates. A machine can be used to reduce the input force that is needed to lift an object. By changing the position of the applied force, load, and fulcrum of a lever the mechanical advantage of the system is changed.

There are three classes of levers that are determined based on the position and direction of the applied force, resultant force, and the fulcrum. Pliers would be considered two connecting first-class levers. A wheelbarrow would be considered a second-class lever. A mousetrap would be considered a third-class lever.

Like everything, you can not get something for anything and energy is no different when it comes to a machine. **You can only get the same amount of energy out of a machine as you put into the machine.** Any energy you put into a system is equal to the energy you get out of that system. With friction, some of the input energy is converted into heat and sound. Because of friction, some of the input energy is lost and the amount of energy that is actual used to do work determines the efficiency of the machine.

Energy is the product of an applied force through a distance. With a lever, when one force is smaller than another force, the smaller force must travel a greater distance than the larger force so that the energy input on the system is equal to the output energy of the system. When the mechanical advantage is greater than 1, the input force (applied force) is smaller than the output force (resultant force) and the applied force is applied over a greater distance than the load's travel distance. When the mechanical advantage is less than 1, the input force is greater than the output force and the load travels a greater distance than the effort force's distance of travel.

Changing the diameter of either the wheel(s) or the axle controls the mechanical advantage of a wheel-axle system. When the ratios of the length of string used per turn divided by the distance traveled is less than 1, the mechanical advantage is small and the car travels slow and far. When the ratios of the length of string used per turn divided by the distance traveled is greater than 1 the car accelerates very quickly and uses only a small amount of string.

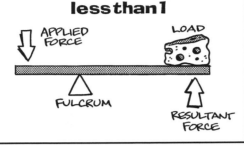

Mechanical Advantage less than 1

APPLIED FORCE

LOAD

FULCRUM

RESULTANT FORCE

Mechanical Advantage greater than 1

APPLIED FORCE

LOAD

FULCRUM

RESULTANT FORCE

Mechanical Advantage

Transmission

The diameters of your drive wheel and drive axle represent your **gearing** or **transmission**. A transmission is any device that transmits mechanical energy from one place to another. With a mouse-trap car, power is transferred to the wheels via the transmission. In addition to getting energy from one place to another, the transmission can be used to trade speed for torque or torque for speed. Some of the common ways to transfer power to the drive wheels are direct drive, gear drive, belt drive, and friction drive. Not all are best used on a mouse-trap car. Gear and pulley ratios are used to describe the mechanical advantage. One gear or pulley is called the "drive" and the other the "driven." The diameter or **ratio** of the drive and driven components of a transmission determines the force and speed that will result. Obviously, there are trade-offs that

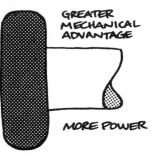

GREATER
MECHANICAL
ADVANTAGE

MORE POWER

LESS
MECHANICAL
ADVANTAGE

LESS
POWER

you need to understand. When a large gear or pulley is driven by a smaller gear or pulley, there is an increase in torque and a decrease in top speed. When a smaller gear or pulley is driven by a larger gear or pulley, there is a decrease in torque and an increase in top speed. Think of pedaling a multispeed bike. When the rear gear on a bike is as small as possible (i.e., it's in high gear), the bike can go the fastest on a level road, but as the road begins to slant upwards the bike begins to slow. More torque is required to propel the bike up the hill. By putting the bike into a lower gear, you increase the mechanical advantage of your gearing and consequently get more torque, but at the cost of less speed. It is important to match your transmission with the activity you need to perform. A Formula 1 race car and a tractor both have transmissions designed for the tasks they perform. A tractor needs more torque than a race car

94

IF LARGE GEAR IS THE DRIVER...
• LESS MECHANICAL ADVANTAGE
• MORE SPEED
• LESS TORQUE

IF THE SMALL GEAR IS THE DRIVER...
• GREATER MECHANICAL ADVANTAGE
• LESS SPEED
• MORE TORQUE

Mechanical Advantage

but with the trade-off of speed. Test your mouse-trap car by running the car in your hand. If you place your vehicle on the ground and the mouse-trap lever does not pull off the start or stops part of the way through its motion, you do not have enough torque. If you do not have enough torque you should increase the mechanical advantage by doing one of the following: making the length of the lever arm smaller, using smaller diameter drive wheels, or using a larger diameter drive axle. The larger the diameter of the driven gear or pulley, the greater the mechanical advantage or torque.

MORE FORCE, BUT LESS PULLING DISTANCE

LESS FORCE, BUT MORE PULLING DISTANCE

DIRECT DRIVE

DRIVE WHEEL

AXLE SHAFT ATTACHED DIRECTLY TO DRIVE WHEEL →

FRICTION DRIVE

FRICTION DISK RUBS DIRECTLY ON DRIVE WHEEL

DRIVE WHEEL

GEAR DRIVE

GEARS

DRIVE WHEEL

BELT DRIVE

DRIVE WHEEL →

BELT

PULLEY

PULLEY

Mechanical Advantage

By increasing or decreasing the wheel-to-axle ratio, you will change the **mechanical advantage** of your mouse-trap car. Keep in mind, changing the **mechanical advantage does not increase the work you get from your mouse trap; it only changes the size of the force and the distance the force is applied**. With distance vehicles, you want a small force over a long distance; therefore, use a large wheel with a small axle (i.e., a large wheel-to-axle ratio). A large wheel with a small axle will cover more distance per each turn of the axle when compared to a smaller wheel with the same axle. There is a trade-off for having a large wheel-to-axle ratio. The trade-off is that it takes more force to accelerate the vehicle to the same speed in the same time as a vehicle that

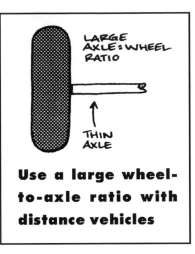

LARGE AXLE:WHEEL RATIO

THIN AXLE

Use a large wheel-to-axle ratio with distance vehicles

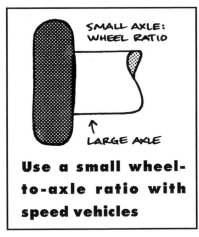

SMALL AXLE: WHEEL RATIO

LARGE AXLE

Use a small wheel-to-axle ratio with speed vehicles

has a small wheel-to-axle ratio, but this is okay because distance cars should not be fast in order to cut down on air resistance. It is essential that a vehicle with a large wheel-to-axle ratio has a small rotational inertia wheel, since low rotational inertia wheels will be much easier to rotate than large rotational inertia wheels.

For quicker accelerations, a large axle size means a larger force is transferred to the ground, causing greater acceleration. By decreasing the wheel-to-axle ratio, you will increase the torque but at the cost of decreasing the distance that the force is being applied. To achieve quicker accelerations with a speed car, use a wheel or wheels with a large axle or a smaller wheel-to-axle ratio than with your distance car. Again, a tapered axle can be designed to distribute larger forces at the start and then decrease the force once the car is in motion.

Mechanical Advantage

Construction Tip

Changing the Torque with Axle Size

MASKING TAPE

↑ DRIVE AXLE

If your vehicle does not have enough torque in order to move off the start, it will not travel the full length of the pulling distance without stopping. Try wrapping **tape** around the drive axle in order to increase the **diameter** and increase the **torque**.

Brain Tip 97

A tapered axle will act like a **transmission** and change the torque or the **gearing** of the drive axle. If you need more torque off the start and less torque towards the end of travel, start winding the string at the thinner part of the gearing so that it starts to unwind from the thicker diameter at the beginning of its travel. If you need more torque towards the end of the vehicle's motion, start winding the string around the thicker part so that it starts to unwind from the smaller diameter.

TAPERED AXLE

TOP VIEW

MORE TORQUE, MORE ACCELERATION

LESS TORQUE, LESS ACCELERATION

Lab #7 - How Far Can I Go?

Purpose

To determine the pulling distance, the power output, and the mechanical advantage.

Equipment Needed

Ruler (A caliper makes smaller measurements easier)
Stopwatch
Meter Tape

Variables Needed From Other Labs

Total Potential Energy from Lab #5

Discussion

The pulling distance is the measurement from where the vehicle starts to where the pulling force on the drive axle ends. In this lab you will calculate how far your mousetrap car should be pulled by the mousetrap's lever arm. Once you have predicted the pulling distance you will then measure and time the actual pulling distance in order to find the power rating. The pulling distance does not tell you how far your mousetrap car will travel, only how far it will be pulled by the mousetrap's lever arm. The distance that your mousetrap car is pulled is directly proportional to the size of the drive wheels and the length of string that is wrapped around the drive axle. The travel distance is inversely proportional to the size of the drive axle. What all this means is the following: the larger the drive wheel(s), the greater the pulling distance. The more string that can be pulled off the drive axle, the greater the pulling distance. The larger the drive axle, the shorter the pulling distance. In order to get more string wound around the drive axle, you can do one of the following: use a smaller diameter drive axle or extend the length of the mousetrap's lever arm and then place the trap further from the drive axle.

Power Output, Gear Ratio, Mechanical Advantage

The pulling distance is calculated from the number of turns that your wheel makes times the circumference of your wheel. The number of turns that your wheel will make depends on the length of string wound around the pulling axle divided by the circumference of the drive axle. By putting the first two formulas together you can predict the pulling distance.

Power Output

Power is the rate at which work is being done. Your mousetrap car will convert stored potential energy from the wound-up spring into work to overcome friction. The rate at which your mousetrap car converts this stored energy into work is your vehicles power rating. You will calculate the power rating by dividing the starting energy by the time through the pulling distance (Formula #4). As a general rule of thumb, higher power ratings mean less efficiency and less overall travel distance. A good mousetrap car that is designed for distance should have a low power rating.

Power Output, Gear Ratio, Mechanical Advantage

Formulas

$$\text{Pulling Distance} = \text{Number of Turns} \times 2\pi r_{wheel}$$

$$\text{Number of Turns} = \frac{\text{Length of String}}{2\pi r_{axle}}$$

$$\text{Pulling Distance} = \frac{\text{Length of String} \times r_{wheel}}{r_{axle}}$$

$$P_1 = \frac{PE_{total}}{\Delta t_1}$$

Power is the rate at which energy is being used

How it Works:

A caliper is used to measure the thickness of the drive axle in order to calculate the diameter. For a more accurate calculation of the diameter of the drive axle two measurements will be taken, without string and with string.

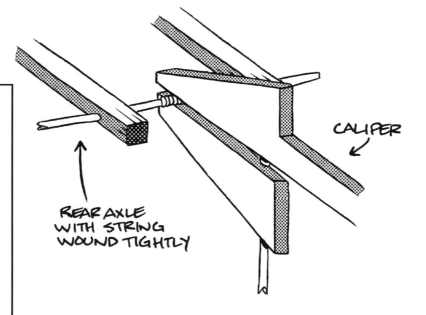

CALIPER

REAR AXLE WITH STRING WOUND TIGHTLY

Power Output, Gear Ratio, Mechanical Advantage

Getting The Measurements

Step 1: Use a caliper or micrometer to measure and calculate the average diameter of the drive axle. Calculate the average diameter of the drive axle by first measuring the drive axle without string on it and then measuring it with string wound-up as it will normally be before a race. It is important that the string be wound evenly and not "balled" or "clumped." Add the two measurements together and then divide by 2. This will give you an average diameter for your calculations. Calculate the average radius from the average diameter.

Ave Drive Axle Diameter = _____ meters

Ave Drive Axle Radius = _____ meters

Step 2: Use a caliper or a ruler to measure the diameter of the drive wheel(s) and record the diameters as well as the radii.

Drive Wheel(s) Diameter = _____ meters

Drive Wheel(s) Radius = _____ meters

Step 3: Measure only the length of string that is normally pulled from the drive axle. Important: If there is more string attached to the lever arm than is needed, you may have to wind the string around the drive axle and then mark the string where it starts and ends with respect to the lever arm's travel range.

String Length = _____ meters

Power Output, Gear Ratio, Mechanical Advantage

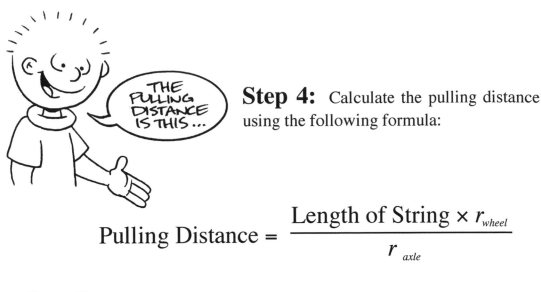

Step 4: Calculate the pulling distance using the following formula:

$$\text{Pulling Distance} = \frac{\text{Length of String} \times r_{wheel}}{r_{axle}}$$

Step 5: Calculate the mechanical advantage from the following formula

$$\frac{F_{\text{Force string applies to drive axle}}}{F_{\text{Force of wheel to road}}} = \frac{r_{\text{radius of wheel}}}{r_{\text{radius of drive axle}}} = \frac{d_{\text{Distance vehicle is pulled by lever arm}}}{d_{\text{String on axle}}} = \text{IMA}$$

Part II   Determine Power Output
Step 6: Time your vehicle over the pulling distance. Perform 3 to 5 trials. Record your data in the data table.

Data Table #1

Pulling Distance	Total Travel Distance	Time Over Pulling Distance	Starting Energy from Lab #2	Power Output
$d_1=$	Total $d_1=$	$t_1=$	PE $=$	$P_1=$
$d_2=$	Total $d_2=$	$t_2=$	PE $=$	$P_2=$
$d_3=$	Total $d_3=$	$t_3=$	PE $=$	$P_3=$
Ave d=		Ave t=		Ave P=

Power Output, Gear Ratio, Mechanical Advantage

Step 7: Calculate the power by dividing the total starting energy from Lab #2 by the time over the pulling distance. Compare your value to other vehicles' power.

$$P_1 = \frac{PE_{total}}{\Delta t_1} \qquad\qquad P_2 = \frac{PE_{total}}{\Delta t_2}$$

Graphing the Results

1. Make a graph of the Power Rating vs. total travel distance. Put "power" on the horizontal axis and "distance" on the vertical axis.
2. Make a graph of Pulling Distance vs. Mechanical Advantage. Put "mechanical advantage" on the horizontal axis and "pulling distance" on the vertical axis.

Analysis

1. Describe any relationship that might exist between power rating and travel distance.
2. Describe any relationship that might exist between wheel to axle ratio and pulling distance.

DID YOU KNOW? ... THE HUMAN BRAIN MAINTAINS ENOUGH POWER TO LIGHT A 10 WATT LIGHT BULB

Power Output, Gear Ratio, Mechanical Advantage

Lab #8 - Conserving Energy

Purpose

In this activity you will calculate the efficiency of your mousetrap car

Materials

Ruler
Caliper
Stopwatch

Variables needed from other labs

Total Potential Energy from Lab #5
Rolling Friction from Lab #6
Coefficient of Rolling Friction from Lab #6
Rotational Inertia for each Wheel or Axle System from Lab #4

Discussion

In this lab you will calculate the overall efficiency of your vehicle. Efficiency is how effectively a machine can transform energy into work without losing energy to friction. It is a rule of nature that in all transformations of energy some energy will be lost to the surroundings because of friction. More efficient machines lose less energy to friction. Efficiency allows you to see just how much of your energy is being used as designed. A mousetrap car uses energy to change speed and displace its position. With a slow-moving distance car, you would expect a more efficient vehicle to travel further than a less efficient car. With a distance car the objective is to reduce friction to a minimum, thereby increasing distance to a maximum.

With a speed car, the objective is to quickly transform the stored potential energy into energy of motion. For a speed car you can measure the efficiency by comparing the starting potential energy to the ending kinetic energy as

Conservation of Energy

Lets Get Rolling

NO PROBLEM!

the vehicle crosses the finish line. The kinetic energy will be stored in two forms: rotational kinetic energy and linear kinetic energy. Rotational kinetic energy is the energy that is in the rotation of the wheels. Linear kinetic energy is in the movement of the car. These two forms of kinetic energy have to be calculated independently and then added together in order to find the total energy at the finish.

EXPERIMENT

Finding the Rolling Friction

Step 1: Use the information from Lab # 2 and record your mousetrap cars starting potential energy .

Total Starting Energy = _____ Joules

105

Data Table #1

Pulling Distance	Time	Final Velocity	Linear Kinetic Energy	Total Rotational Energy	Total Kinetic Energy	Work Done	Efficiency
$d_1=$	$t_1=$	$v_1=$	$KE_{tran\,1}=$	$KE_{rot\,1}=$	$KE_1=$	$w_1=$	$E_1=$
$d_2=$	$t_2=$	$v_2=$	$KE_{tran\,2}=$	$KE_{rot\,2}=$	$KE_2=$	$w_2=$	$E_2=$
$d_3=$	$t_3=$	$v_3=$	$KE_{tran\,3}=$	$KE_{rot\,3}=$	$KE_3=$	$w_3=$	$E_3=$
$d_4=$	$t_4=$	$v_4=$	$KE_{tran\,4}=$	$KE_{rot\,4}=$	$KE_4=$	$w_4=$	$E_4=$
AVE	$d=$	$h=$	$KE_{tran}=$	$KE_{rot}=$	$KE=$	$w=$	$E=$

Step 2: Place your mousetrap car on the start line Walk along side of your mousetrap car and measure the pulling distance. You can also use the data you calculated from Lab #3: *Predicting Pulling Distance*. Record the pulling distance in Data Table #1 under "Pulling Distance. "

Conservation of Energy

Step 3: Place your mousetrap car on the start line. Release the mousetrap car and time it over the pulling distance only. **Do not time beyond the pulling distance**. Test three to five times and record in Data Table #1 under "Time."

Step 4: Use the following formula to calculate the final velocities for each trial. Record your results in Data Table #1 under "Final velocity."

$$\text{Final Velocity} = \frac{2 * \text{Pulling Distance}}{\text{Time}}$$

Step 5: Find the mass for your vehicle so that you can calculate the linear kinetic energy. Calculate the linear kinetic energy for each trial using the mass times the final velocity squared. Record your answer under "Linear Kinetic Energy" in Data Table #1.

$$KE_{tran_1} = \frac{(m) * (V_{f_1})^2}{2}$$

Finding the Rotational Kinetic Energy

Step 6: From Lab#5 record the rotational inertia for each wheel or axle system in data table #2. Also record the radius for each wheel on your vehicle.

Data Table #2

	Front Wheel #1 Or Front Axle System	Front Wheel #2	Rear Wheel #1 Or Rear Axle System	Rear Wheel #2
Rotational Inertia	$I_{f1} =$	$I_{f2} =$	$I_{r1} =$	$I_{r2} =$
Radius of Wheel	$r_{f1} =$	$r_{f2} =$	$r_{r1} =$	$r_{r2} =$

Conservation of Energy

Step 7: Using the final velocities from Table #1, calculate the rotational kinetic energy for each trial. You must calculate each wheel or axle system separately.

$$KE\,1_{rot_1} = \frac{(I)*(v_{f_1})^2}{2*(r_1)^2}$$

Data Table #3

Trial #	KE_{rot} Wheel #1	KE_{rot} Wheel #2	KE_{rot} Wheel #3	KE_{rot} Wheel #4	Total Rotational Kinetic Energy
1=	$KE\,1_{rot\,1}=$	$KE\,2_{rot\,1}=$	$KE\,3_{rot\,1}=$	$KE\,4_{rot\,1}=$	$KE_{rot\,1}=$
2=	$KE\,1_{rot\,2}=$	$KE\,2_{rot\,2}=$	$KE\,3_{rot\,2}=$	$KE\,4_{rot\,2}=$	$KE_{rot\,2}=$
3=	$KE\,1_{rot\,3}=$	$KE\,2_{rot\,3}=$	$KE\,3_{rot\,3}=$	$KE\,4_{rot\,3}=$	$KE_{rot\,3}=$
4=	$KE\,1_{rot\,4}=$	$KE\,2_{rot\,4}=$	$KE\,3_{rot\,4}=$	$KE\,4_{rot\,4}=$	$KE_{rot\,4}=$

Step 8: Once you have found the rotational kinetic energy for each wheel, add each value together for each trial in order to get the total rotational kinetic energy, record in Data Table #3 and then transfer the Total Rotational Kinetic Energy to Table #1.

$$KE_{rot_1} = KE\,1_{rot_1} + KE\,2_{rot_1} + KE\,3_{rot_1} + KE\,4_{rot_1}$$

Step 9: From Table #1 add the linear kinetic energy with the total rotational kinetic energy. This value represents the total energy of your vehicle when all the potential energy is converted into kinetic energy.

$$KE_1 = KE_{rot_1} + KE_{tran_1}$$

Conservation of Energy

Step 10: Subtract the total kinetic energy from the starting potential energy to get the work lost to friction.

$$W_1 = PE_1 - KE_1$$

Step 11: With a distance vehicle the objective is to convert the starting potential energy into distance by doing work to overcome friction. With a speed car the objective is to convert the starting potential energy into kinetic energy. Calculate the efficiency for your vehicle by dividing the total kinetic energy by the starting potential energy and then multiplying by 100 in order to get a percentage.

$$\text{Efficiency}_1 = \frac{KE_1}{PE_{start}} * 100$$

Step 12: Calculate the amount of rolling friction acting against your vehicle using the energy lost to friction or the work divided by the pulling distance.

$$f_1 = \frac{W_1}{d_1}$$

Conservation of Energy

Graphing the Results

You will now graph your data in order to learn from your results. In each of the following graphs, attempt to draw a "best fit" line. If data is widely scattered, do not attempt to connect each dot but instead draw the best line you can that represents the shape of the dots. If you have access to a computer, you can use a spread sheet like Microsoft Exel to plot your data.

1. Graph **Pulling Distance** vs. **Work** for each vehicle in the class.

2. Graph **Pulling Distance** vs **Efficiency** for each vehicle in the class.

Analysis

1. Explain how pulling distance is related to energy lost to friction or the work done.

2. Explain the relationship that exists between pulling distance and efficiency.

Torque

KNOB IS
PLACED TOO
CLOSE TO
HINGES

When you turn a water faucet, open a door, or tighten a nut with a wrench, you exert a turning force called a **torque**. Torque is the rotational counterpart of **force**. You apply a force to make an object move or accelerate in a particular direction. You apply a torque to make an object turn or rotate. A torque is produced when a force is exerted with **leverage**. For example, a doorknob is on the opposite side of the door from the hinges in order to increase the leverage. By placing the doorknob far from the turning axis of the hinges, less force is required when you push or pull on the doorknob. Less effort is required to use a long wrench than a short wrench to loosen a nut because you have more leverage with a long handle. The distance from the turning axis to the point of contact is called the **lever arm** when the force is applied perpendicularly. Therefore, torque is the product of the lever arm and the force that tends to produce rotation. It is important to note the direction of your applied force. You push or pull the doorknob **perpendicular** to the plane of the door.

Physics Rules!

110

As the lever arm begins to pull the vehicle, the angle of the pulling force will change with the lever arm until the pulling angle is "zero," at which point the lever arm will fall quickly without any tension in the string.

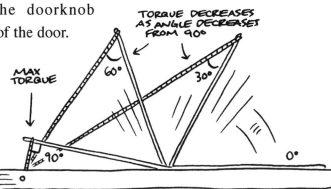

TORQUE DECREASES
AS ANGLE DECREASES
FROM 90°

MAX
TORQUE

60°

30°

90°

0°

Torque

The key to a quick start is the proper relationship between the **tension on the string** and the **grip friction of the tires**. If the pulling force on the string is too large, the tires will spin at the start, wasting the spring's energy and thus decreasing performance. The tension of the pulling

TIE STRING ABOVE THE DRIVE AXLE

string should be at its maximum for a speed vehicle but not large enough to cause the wheels to spin off the start. By adjusting the length of the mouse trap's lever arm, you can vary the force that is applied to the wheels of your car. Long lever arms decrease the pulling force while short arms increase the pulling force.

Upon release, energy will be wasted if the arm is not properly positioned. The pulling string must pull perpendicular to the axle's radius for maximum performance at the start! Lever arms should not extend past the axle when in the lowered position.

For distance cars, the tension on the pulling string should be just enough to start the car rolling and maintain a

somewhat constant motion throughout its journey, adjust the lever arm to the point where the mouse-trap car almost stops moving. The longer the length of the lever arm that you use, the more string you can wind around the drive axle. Therefore, a greater overall travel distance can occur as the string is pulled off the drive axle. Less pulling force is transferred to the wheels when a long lever arm is used. For this reason, you must reduce the required pulling force by reducing friction and rotational inertia to the absolute minimum.

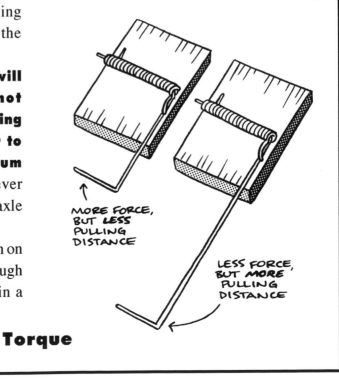

MORE FORCE, BUT LESS PULLING DISTANCE

LESS FORCE, BUT MORE PULLING DISTANCE

Torque

Construction Tip
Trap Placement

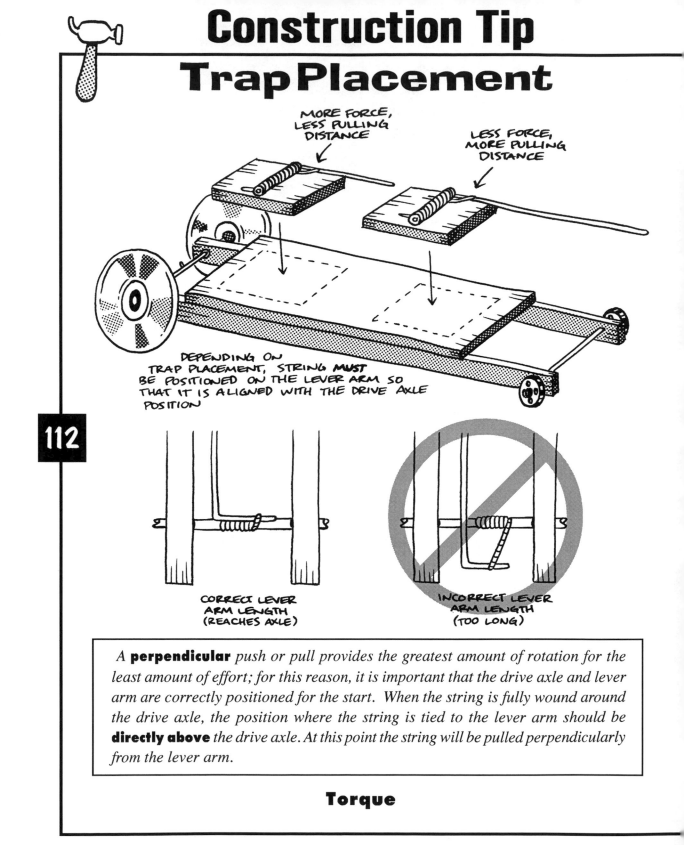

MORE FORCE, LESS PULLING DISTANCE

LESS FORCE, MORE PULLING DISTANCE

DEPENDING ON TRAP PLACEMENT, STRING **MUST** BE POSITIONED ON THE LEVER ARM SO THAT IT IS ALIGNED WITH THE DRIVE AXLE POSITION

CORRECT LEVER ARM LENGTH (REACHES AXLE)

INCORRECT LEVER ARM LENGTH (TOO LONG)

A **perpendicular** push or pull provides the greatest amount of rotation for the least amount of effort; for this reason, it is important that the drive axle and lever arm are correctly positioned for the start. When the string is fully wound around the drive axle, the position where the string is tied to the lever arm should be **directly above** the drive axle. At this point the string will be pulled perpendicularly from the lever arm.

Torque

Construction Tip

Changing the Length of the Lever Arm

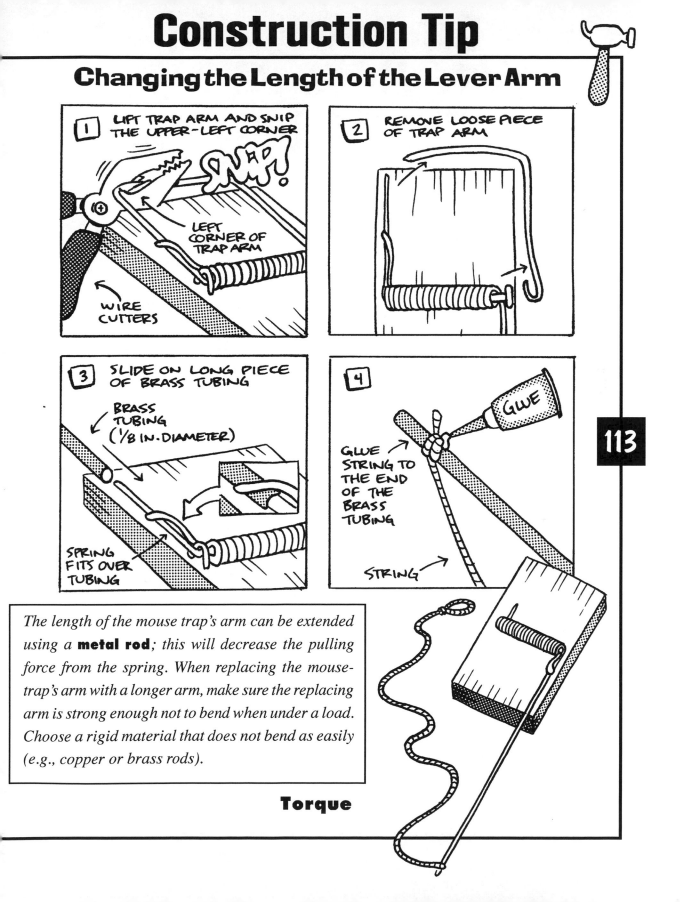

1. LIFT TRAP ARM AND SNIP THE UPPER-LEFT CORNER

SNAP!

LEFT CORNER OF TRAP ARM

WIRE CUTTERS

2. REMOVE LOOSE PIECE OF TRAP ARM

3. SLIDE ON LONG PIECE OF BRASS TUBING

BRASS TUBING (1/8 IN. DIAMETER)

SPRING FITS OVER TUBING

4. GLUE

GLUE STRING TO THE END OF THE BRASS TUBING

STRING

*The length of the mouse trap's arm can be extended using a **metal rod**; this will decrease the pulling force from the spring. When replacing the mouse-trap's arm with a longer arm, make sure the replacing arm is strong enough not to bend when under a load. Choose a rigid material that does not bend as easily (e.g., copper or brass rods).*

Torque

Construction Tip
Attaching the Trap

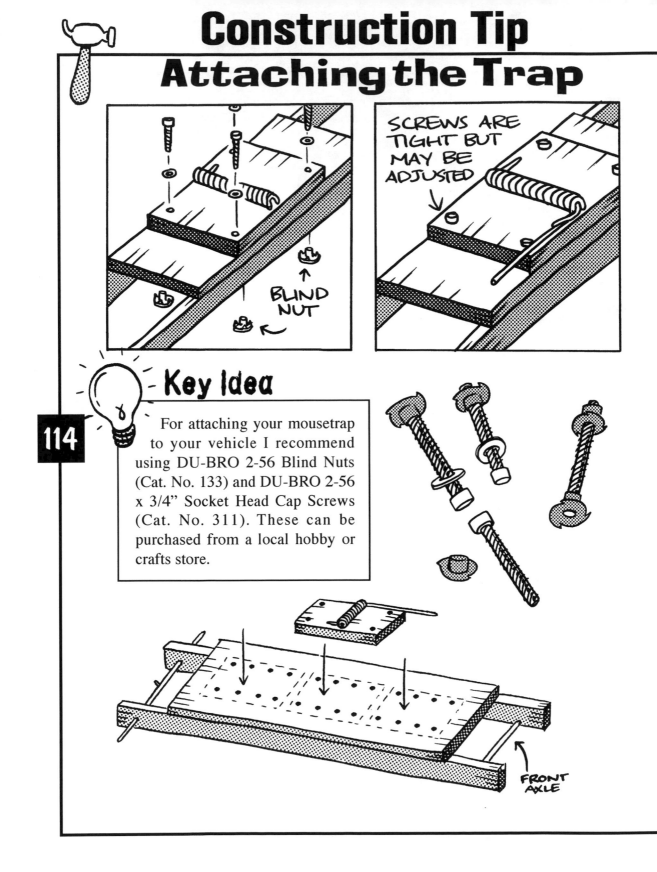

SCREWS ARE TIGHT BUT MAY BE ADJUSTED

BLIND NUT

Key Idea

For attaching your mousetrap to your vehicle I recommend using DU-BRO 2-56 Blind Nuts (Cat. No. 133) and DU-BRO 2-56 x 3/4" Socket Head Cap Screws (Cat. No. 311). These can be purchased from a local hobby or crafts store.

FRONT AXLE

Construction Tip
Attaching the Trap

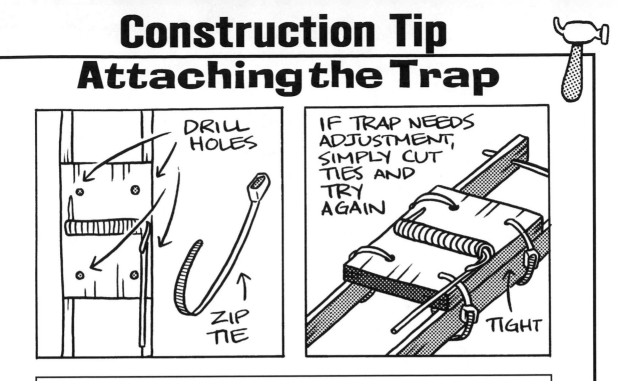

DRILL HOLES

ZIP TIE

IF TRAP NEEDS ADJUSTMENT, SIMPLY CUT TIES AND TRY AGAIN

TIGHT

If your frame does not have a deck top, you can try using **ZIP-TIES** *to hold the mousetrap to the frame. Drill four holes in the corners of the mousetrap that are large enough to thread the* **ZIP-TIES** *through, then place the mouse trap on the frame and tighten* **ZIP-TIES** *in place. If you want to try placing the mousetrap in a new location, just cut the* **ZIP-TIES** *and relocate the along the frame.*

It is **important** that you **test** the mousetrap in many different locations before you decide on a final placement. Try drilling a series of holes along the vehicle and then anchoring the mousetrap with some nuts and bolts or try using a **ZIP-TIE to** hold the mousetrap to the frame, with either method it is easy to remove the mousetrap and reposition it to anew location.

Brain Tip

Key Ideas you should consider when building a good distance vehicle

- **Longer lever arms** The more string that can be pulled off the drive axle translates into more turns that the wheels can make, this causes your vehicle to cover more distance under the pulling force.

TRAP

- **Large Drive Wheel(s)** Large drive wheels cover more linear distance for each rotation than a smaller diameter wheel. The best wheels tend to be between 1-2 feet in diam-eter.

- **Small Drive Axle** You can get more turns with a smaller axle for the same length of string than with a larger one. More turns of the axle means more turns of the wheel, which means greater travel distance.

- **Small Power Output** Vehicles that move slower tend to be more energy efficient in comparison to an equally built car of same rolling friction. You can slow a car down by increasing the lever arm length and repositioning the mousetrap further from the drive axle. At low speeds, air resistance is not a large factor in the motion of a moving object, but as the speed of an object increases, the force of air resistance also increases; therefore, at higher speeds moving objects will have to expend more energy to maintain constant velocity. For this reason, it is best to build a slow moving distance car!

Distance Car

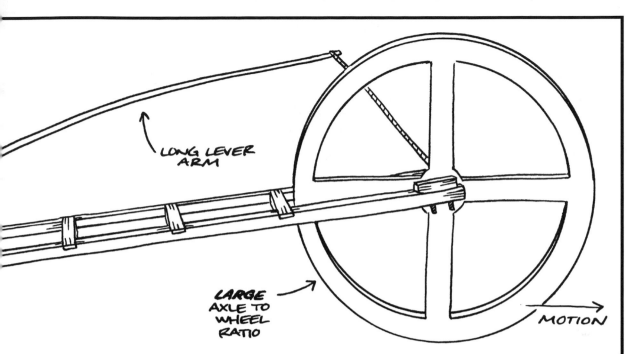

LONG LEVER ARM

LARGE → AXLE TO WHEEL RATIO

MOTION

Decrease Mass and Rotational Inertia Build a lightweight frame and use lightweight wheels. Remove mass from wheels to decrease rotational inertia.

- **Sample Different Mousetraps** Not all mousetrap springs have the same spring tension. The greater the tension in a mousetrap, the more energy you will be able to store when the spring is wound-up.

- **Remove ALL Friction** This one is impossible but the more you can reduce friction, the less energy that will be lost to heat and sound which translates into greater travel distance. Your vehicle should have the lowest possible energy consumption; this means that your vehicle should be a slow mover and use ball bearings.

Using these principles, mouse-trap cars have traveled 100[+] meters!

Distance Car

Ideas for Increasing Distance

1   *Decrease rolling friction by re-working the friction points. Polish bushings or use ball bearings. If you are using bearings, soak them in WD-40; this will remove any oil or grease. Although grease and oil are lubricants and often used to reduce friction, adding them to mouse-trap car bearings slows the car down because of the large viscosity of the lubricants.*

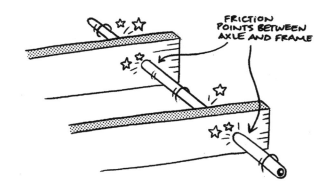

FRICTION POINTS BETWEEN AXLE AND FRAME

2   *Decrease the force required to pull the vehicle by decreasing the rotational inertia. Decrease the rotational inertia by removing mass from the inside of the wheels. Decrease the overall mass of the car by removing mass from the frame and use a light-weight lever arm. Move the trap away from the pulling axle and extend the lever arm. Re-adjust the string and the string attachment point. Don not add mass around the outside of wheels such as rubber bands or balloons.*

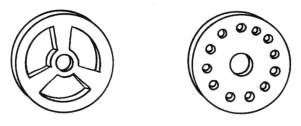

3   *Use a larger drive wheel. Try making a wheel out of mat board. Mat board is stiff and light weight.*

Distance Car

4 *Use a smaller drive axle. The larger the ratio of drive wheel(s)-to-axle(s) diameter, the farther you car will go for each turn of the wheel and the greater the pulling distance will be.*

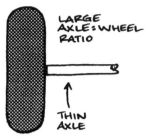

5 *Find a stronger mouse trap. Test different mouse traps in order to find the strongest one.*

6 *If your car is stopping and the spring is not at its resting point, find a stronger mouse trap or try to make a tapered axle so you can change the torque required to turn the wheels as the pulling force to the drive axle changes, or build up the drive axle with tape.*

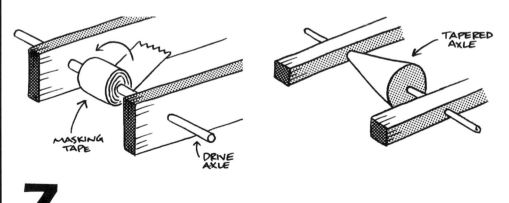

7 *Check string alignment and make sure that the string is attached directly over the drive axle with the lever arm held in the fully wound position.*

Distance Car

119

Building the Perfect Speed Cars

Brain Tip

Key Ideas you should consider when building a good speed vehicle. Using these principles, I have seen mouse-trap cars travel 5 meters in under 1 second!

- **Shorter lever arms** shorter lever arms have more pulling force, more pulling force means greater acceleration, greater acceleration mean less time before the vehicle reaches top speed. If the lever arm is too short your vehicle will slip off the start and will waste energy. Therefore, adjust the lever length in order to find the best performance

- **Smaller Drive Wheel(s)** Wheels should be around 2-5 inches in diameter but no larger than a compact disc. If the wheel-to-axle ratio too small your vehicle will slip off the start and will waste energy. Therefore, adjust the ratio in order to find the best performance

- **Increase the Traction** Use rubber bands on the drive wheels and/or Traction Action® on the wheels in order to increase the traction. More traction means greater acceleration.

- **Larger Diameter Drive Axle** You can get more torque with a thick axle. More torque means greater acceleration! You can build the axle up with tape to increases the axle diameter.

- **Large Power Output** The vehicle should be designed to have a large energy consumption in a short period of time (i.e., a large power output). A vehicle that can get-up to its top speed as fast as possible will have a shorter time over a timed distance. With a car designed for speed , the objective is how quickly can the vehicle convert its potential energy into kinetic energy.

Speed Car

- **Decrease Mass and Rotational Inertia** MORE IMPORTANT WITH A SPEED CAR THAN A DISTANCE VEHICLE. Build a lightweight frame and use lightweight wheels. A wheel with a large rotational inertia can really limit a cars performance, remove as much mass as possible from wheels to decrease rotational inertia.

- **Sample Different Mousetraps** Not all mousetrap springs have the same spring tension. The greater the tension in a mousetrap, the more energy you will be able to store when the spring is wound-up.

- **Remove ALL Friction** This one is impossible but the more you can reduce friction, the less energy that will be lost to heat and sound, which translates into greater speed. Your vehicle should have the lowest possible energy consumption do to friction; this means that your vehicle should use ball bearings.

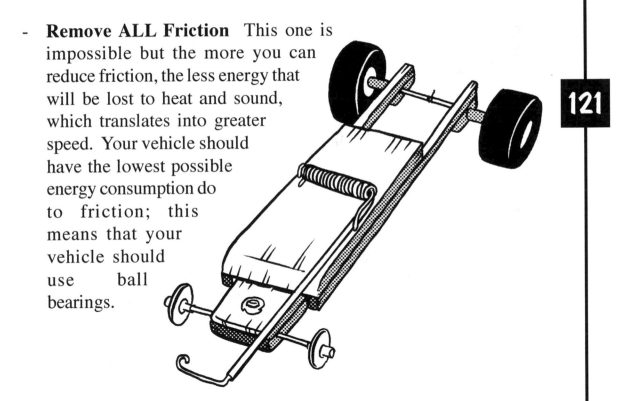

Speed Car

Ideas for Increasing Speed

1 *Move the mouse trap closer to the drive axle as long as the wheels are not spinning and decrease lever arm accordingly.*

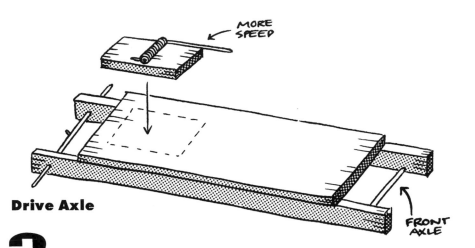

MORE SPEED

Drive Axle

FRONT AXLE

2 *Increase traction on drive wheels by using rubber bands or the middle section of a rubber balloon around the drive wheels. Try adding mass directly above the drive axle.*

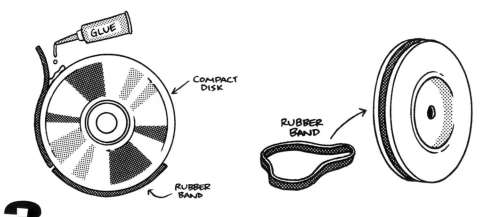

GLUE

COMPACT DISK

RUBBER BAND

RUBBER BAND

3 *Move the trap away from drive wheel(s) **only if the wheels are slipping**. This will decrease the pulling force which is the reason for the slipping wheels.*

Speed Car

4 *Decrease rolling friction by re-working the friction points. Polish bushings or use ball bearings. If you are using bearings, soak them in WD-40l; this will remove any oil or grease. Although grease and oil are lubricants and often used to reduce friction, adding them to mouse-trap car bearings slows the car down because of the large viscosity of the lubricants.*

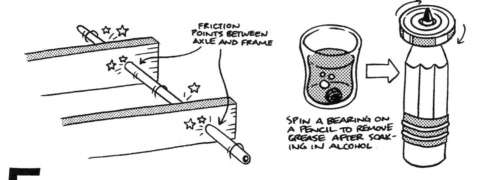

FRICTION POINTS BETWEEN AXLE AND FRAME

SPIN A BEARING ON A PENCIL TO REMOVE GREASE AFTER SOAKING IN ALCOHOL

5 *Decrease rotational inertia of wheels by removing mass from the inside of the wheels. Also, try smaller diameter wheels.*

6 *Adjust the wheel-to-axle ratio by adding or removing tape on the drive axle.*

SMALL AXLE: WHEEL RATIO

LARGE AXLE

MASKING TAPE

DRIVE AXLE

7 *Check string alignment and make sure that the string is attached directly over the drive axle with the lever arm held in the fully wound position.*

Speed Car

PROBLEM:

Axle slides back and forth causing wheels to rub against the frame of the car, slowing or stopping the car.

1. Add thrust washer between wheels and the frame for a smoother rubbing surface with less friction.

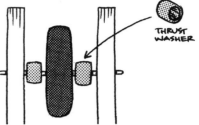

THRUST WASHER

2. Make spacers out of brass tubing to hold the wheels in place and limit the side-to-side play of the wheels or axles.
3. If you are using bearings, the axle may be moving side to side. Carefully glue the axles to the bearings without getting glue in the bearings.

124

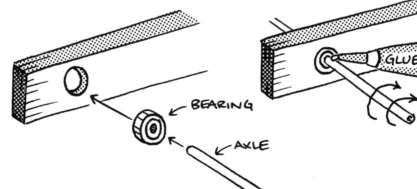

GLUE

BEARING

AXLE

PROBLEM:

Can't find an axle to fit the wheels or bearings.

1. Re-size the axle or change the wheel's hole size with a spacer.

¼ L SINK WASHER USED AS A WHEEL SPACER

PROBLEM:

Mouse trap falls quickly but car moves slowly.

1. Drive wheels are not glued to the axle and the axle is spinning inside the wheels. Glue wheels to axle.

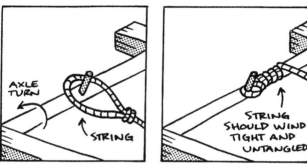

2. There is no hook on the axle for attaching the string and/or the string is slipping off the axle without pulling. The hook may not be glued to the axle and is slipping under the tension of the string.

PROBLEM:

Mouse trap car does not start or moves slowly.

1. Too much friction in the rolling points. Re-do the rolling points or try ball bearings.

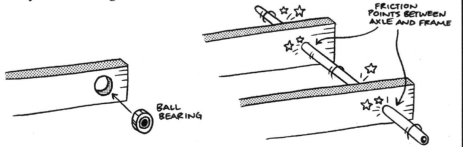

Technical Help

PROBLEM:

Mouse trap car does not start or moves slowly. (Continued)

2. Not enough tension in the pulling string. Move the trap closer to the drive axle and adjust the string attachment point on the lever arm accordingly *or* try to build up the drive axle with tape. Lastly, test different mouse traps and use the strongest one.

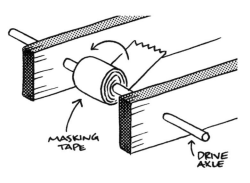

PROBLEM:

Mouse trap car does not travel straight.

1. Wheels are not pointing in the same direction. The solution is to bring the wheels into alignment. If the vehicle is a three-wheeled vehicle you need to focus your efforts on the single wheel. Try to align it with the other two. This is not easy!

2. This only applies to long distance cars that use one large wheel as the drive wheel. If the car travels straight when you push it without the tension of the lever arm, but turns once under the pulling tension of the trap, there is too much frame flex or the trap is pulling too hard on one side of the axle. Strengthen the frame or prevent the pulling side of the axle from giving too much at its holding points.

Technical Help

PROBLEM:

Mouse-trap car suddenly stops or slows quickly.

1. The string is not releasing from the drive axle because it is either glued to the axle or it is too long *or* the hook is too long and caching the string causing it to rewind.

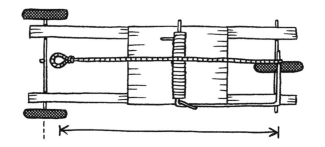

> *Cut string a little bit **shorter** than what is needed in order to insure a proper release.*

2. There is too much friction at the rolling points. Re-work the bearings to reduce friction or try ball bearings. Try a small diameter axle.

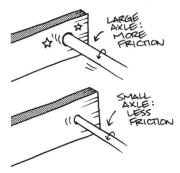

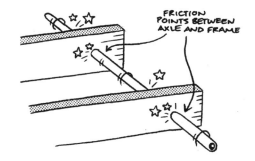

3. Wheels are rubbing on the frame. Prevent wheels from rubbing with spacers or thrust washers.

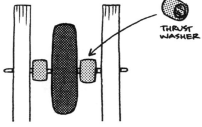

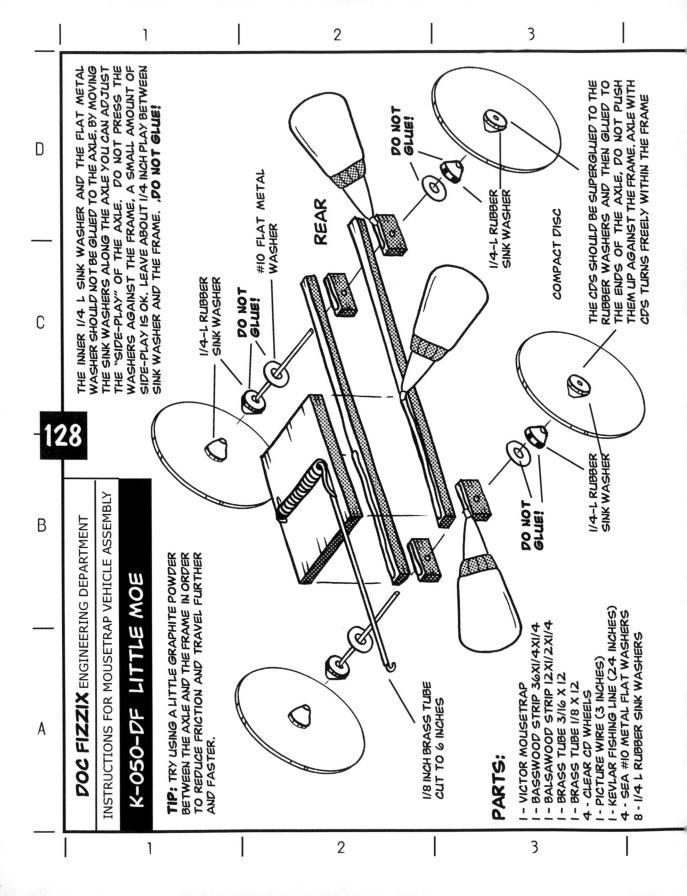

DOC FIZZIX ENGINEERING DEPARTMENT

INSTRUCTIONS FOR MOUSETRAP VEHICLE ASSEMBLY

K-050-DF LITTLE MOE

TIP: TRY USING A LITTLE GRAPHITE POWDER BETWEEN THE AXLE AND THE FRAME IN ORDER TO REDUCE FRICTION AND TRAVEL FURTHER AND FASTER.

128

THE INNER 1/4 L SINK WASHER AND THE FLAT METAL WASHER SHOULD NOT BE GLUED TO THE AXLE. BY MOVING THE SINK WASHERS ALONG THE AXLE YOU CAN ADJUST THE "SIDE-PLAY" OF THE AXLE. DO NOT PRESS THE WASHERS AGAINST THE FRAME, A SMALL AMOUNT OF SIDE-PLAY IS OK. LEAVE ABOUT 1/4 INCH PLAY BETWEEN SINK WASHER AND THE FRAME. **DO NOT GLUE!**

REAR

DO NOT GLUE!

#10 FLAT METAL WASHER

1/4-L RUBBER SINK WASHER

DO NOT GLUE!

1/4-L RUBBER SINK WASHER

COMPACT DISC

THE CD'S SHOULD BE SUPERGLUED TO THE RUBBER WASHERS AND THEN GLUED TO THE ENDS OF THE AXLE, DO NOT PUSH THEM UP AGAINST THE FRAME. AXLE WITH CD'S TURNS FREELY WITHIN THE FRAME

1/4-L RUBBER SINK WASHER

DO NOT GLUE!

1/8 INCH BRASS TUBE CUT TO 6 INCHES

PARTS:

1 - VICTOR MOUSETRAP
1 - BASSWOOD STRIP 36X1/4X1/4
1 - BALSAWOOD STRIP 12X1/2X1/4
1 - BRASS TUBE 3/16 X 12
1 - BRASS TUBE 1/8 X 12
4 - CLEAR CD WHEELS
1 - PICTURE WIRE (3 INCHES)
1 - KEVLAR FISHING LINE (24 INCHES)
4 - SEA #10 METAL FLAT WASHERS
8 - 1/4 L RUBBER SINK WASHERS

GLUING THE FRAME TOGETHER

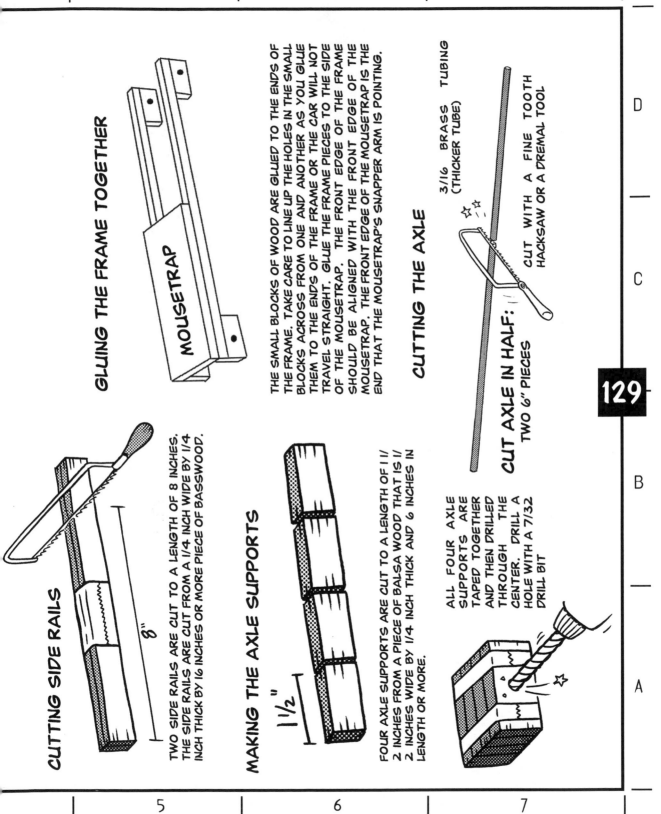

MOUSETRAP

THE SMALL BLOCKS OF WOOD ARE GLUED TO THE ENDS OF THE FRAME. TAKE CARE TO LINE UP THE HOLES IN THE SMALL BLOCKS ACROSS FROM ONE AND ANOTHER AS YOU GLUE THEM TO THE ENDS OF THE FRAME OR THE CAR WILL NOT TRAVEL STRAIGHT. GLUE THE FRAME PIECES TO THE SIDE OF THE MOUSETRAP. THE FRONT EDGE OF THE FRAME SHOULD BE ALIGNED WITH THE FRONT EDGE OF THE MOUSETRAP. THE FRONT EDGE OF THE MOUSETRAP IS THE END THAT THE MOUSETRAP'S SNAPPER ARM IS POINTING.

CUTTING THE AXLE

3/16 BRASS TUBING (THICKER TUBE)

CUT WITH A FINE TOOTH HACKSAW OR A DREMAL TOOL

CUT AXLE IN HALF:
TWO 6" PIECES

CUTTING SIDE RAILS

8"

TWO SIDE RAILS ARE CUT TO A LENGTH OF 8 INCHES. THE SIDE RAILS ARE CUT FROM A 1/4 INCH WIDE BY 1/4 INCH THICK BY 16 INCHES OR MORE PIECE OF BASSWOOD.

MAKING THE AXLE SUPPORTS

1 1/2"

FOUR AXLE SUPPORTS ARE CUT TO A LENGTH OF 1 1/2 INCHES FROM A PIECE OF BALSA WOOD THAT IS 1/2 INCHES WIDE BY 1/4 INCH THICK AND 6 INCHES IN LENGTH OR MORE.

ALL FOUR AXLE SUPPORTS ARE TAPED TOGETHER AND THEN DRILLED THROUGH THE CENTER. DRILL A HOLE WITH A 7/32 DRILL BIT

AXLE SET-UP

THE CDS SHOULD BE SUPERGLUED TO THE RUBBER WASHERS AND THEN GLUED TO THE ENDS OF THE AXLE. DO NOT PUSH THEM UP AGAINST THE FRAME. AXLE WITH CDS TURNS FREELY WITHIN THE FRAME. PLACE THE AXLE THROUGH THE HOLES ON EITHER END OF THE FRAME. PLACE A #10 FLAT METAL WASHER ON EACH SIDE OF THE AXLE. PLACE AND MOVE A 1/4-L RUBBER SINK WASHER DOWN EACH SIDE OF THE AXLE UNTIL THERE IS ABOUT 1/8 - 1/4 INCH SPACING BETWEEN THE METAL WASHER AND THE FRAME. **DO NOT GLUE!**

HOOK & LOOP

ON THE FREE END OF THE STRING TIE A LOOP THAT IS LARGE ENOUGH TO CATCH THE HOOK

HOOK AND LOOP ARE DESIGNED TO RELEASE.

LEVER ARM LENGTH

THE LEVER ARM SHOULD BE LONG ENOUGH TO REACH THE DRIVE AXLE AND **NOT** LONGER OR SHORTER. IF YOU TRY MOUNTING THE MOUSETRAP AT DIFFERENT LOCATIONS FROM THE DRIVE AXLE YOU WILL HAVE TO **ADJUST** THE LENGTH OF THE LEVER ARM AND THE STRING BY CUTTING BOTH. THE STRING SHOULD "JUST" REACH THE DRIVE AXLE OR BE A LITTLE SHORTER SO THAT IT FULLY RELEASES FROM THE AXLE HOOK AND DOES NOT GET TANGLED OR RE-WIND.

MAKING THE AXLE HOOK

TWIST WIRE ON AXLE

TWIST THE SMALL WIRE TIGHTLY AROUND THE DRIVE AXLE (REAR AXLE). **BE CAREFUL!** IF YOU TWIST TOO TIGHT THE WIRE WILL BREAK.

GLUE HOOK TO AXLE

TRIM THE AXLE HOOK WITH A SCISSORS. THE AXLE HOOK SHOULD **NOT** BE LONGER THAN 1/8 INCH.

PUT A COUPLE DROPS OF **SUPERGLUE** ON THE HOOK TO BOND IT WITH THE AXLE.

TIE A LOOP KNOT

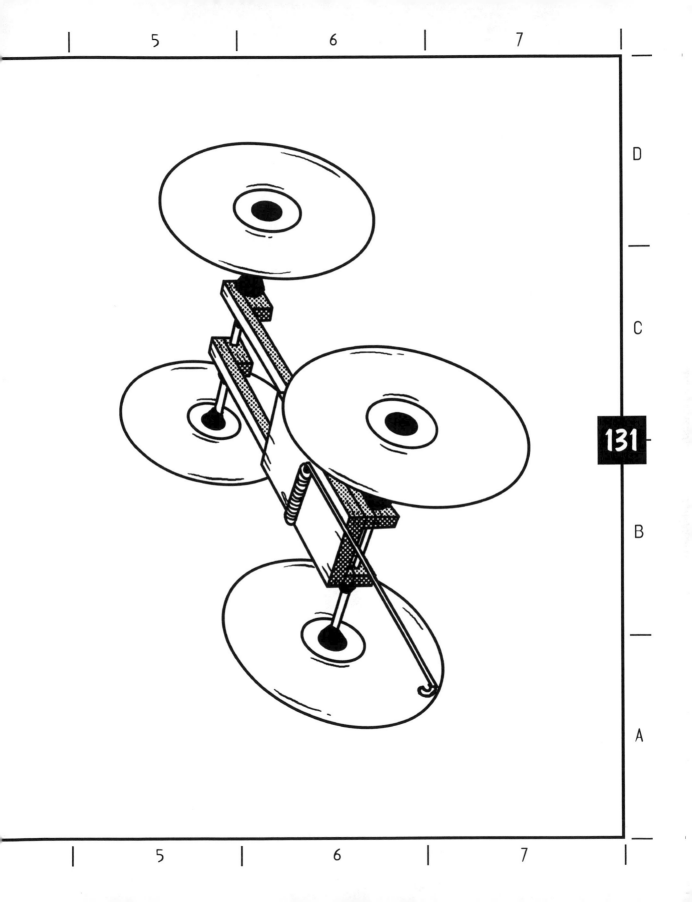

DOC FIZZIX ENGINEERING DEPARTMENT

INSTRUCTIONS FOR MOUSETRAP VEHICLE ASSEMBLY

K-100-DF THE BASIC KIT

1 - VICTOR MOUSETRAP
1 - BALSA STRIP 36X3X3/16
1 - BRASS TUBE 3/16 X 12
1 - BRASS TUBE 1/8 X 12
4 - CLEAR CD WHEELS
1 - PICTURE WIRE (3 INCHES)
1 - KEVLAR FISHING LINE (24 INCHES)
4 - SEA #10 METAL FLAT WASHERS
8 - 1/4 L RUBBER SINK WASHERS

TIP: TRY USING A LITTLE GRAPHITE POWDER BETWEEN THE AXLE AND THE FRAME IN ORDER TO REDUCE FRICTION AND TRAVEL FURTHER AND FASTER.

STRING LENGTH

THE STRING SHOULD BE **"JUST"** LONG ENOUGH TO REACH TO THE DRIVE AXLE'S HOOK. IF THE STRING IS "TOO" LONG IT WILL GET TANGLED. AS A **RULE**, THE STRING SHOULD ONLY BE **TWICE** THE LENGTH OF THE LEVER ARM OR A LITTLE SHORTER

COMPACT DISC

1/4-L RUBBER SINK WASHER

REAR

DO NOT GLUE!

REAR AXLE THICK TUBE CUT TO 6"

1/4-L RUBBER SINK WASHER

#10 FLAT METAL WASHER

DO NOT GLUE!

1/4-L RUBBER SINK WASHER

FRONT

FRONT AXLE THICK TUBE CUT TO 6"

DO NOT GLUE!

1/4-L RUBBER SINK WASHER

THE CDS SHOULD BE SUPERGLUED TO THE RUBBER WASHERS AND THEN GLUED TO THE ENDS OF THE AXLE, DO NOT PUSH THEM UP AGAINST THE FRAME. AXLE WITH CDS TURNS FREELY WITHIN THE FRAME

PLACE THE AXLE THROUGH THE HOLES ON EITHER END OF THE FRAME. PLACE A #10 FLAT METAL WASHER ON EACH SIDE OF THE AXLE. PLACE AND MOVE A 1/4-L RUBBER SINK WASHER DOWN EACH SIDE OF THE AXLE UNTIL THERE IS ABOUT 1/8 - 1/4 INCH SPACING BETWEEN THE METAL WASHER AND THE FRAME. **DO NOT GLUE!**

CUTTING THE AXLE

3/16 BRASS TUBING (THICKER TUBE)

CUT WITH A FINE TOOTH HACKSAW OR A DREMAL TOOL

CUT AXLE IN HALF:
TWO 6" PIECES

SHORTER PIECE 12" X 3"

3"

GLUE

THE DECK TOP SHOULD BE CENTERED 3" FROM EACH END GLUE WITH HOT GLUE OR WHITE ELMER'S GLUE

MORE SPEED

MORE PULLING DISTANCE

FRONT

REAR

10 INCHES MAXIMUM

THESE PLANS ARE DESIGNED SO THAT THE BUILDER CAN MOUNT THE BACK END OF THE MOUSETRAP 10" **MAXIMUM** DISTANCE FROM THE REAR END OF THAT CAR WITHOUT HAVING TO ADJUST THE LENGTH OF THE 12" LEVER ARM.

TAKE A 36" INCH PIECE OF LIGHT WOOD AND CUT IT INTO 12", 18", AND 6" PIECES, AS SHOWN.

18"

6"

12"

DISCARD

DISCARD THE 6" PIECE. MAKE SURE THAT YOUR CUTS ARE CLEAN AND SANDED SO AS TO REDUCE AIR FRICTION. THE 12" PIECE WILL BECOME THE "DECK TOP" AND THE 18" PIECE WILL BECOME THE "SIDE RAILS".

SCORE THE WOOD, USING A METAL RULER AS A GUIDE UNTIL THE WOOD SPLITS EVENLY DOWN THE MIDDLE

METAL RULER

ABOUT 3/4 INCHES FROM THE END

TAPE THE TWO SIDE RAILS TOGETHER. DRILL A HOLE AT EACH END OF THE TWO SIDE RAILS WITH A 7/32 DRILL BIT

133

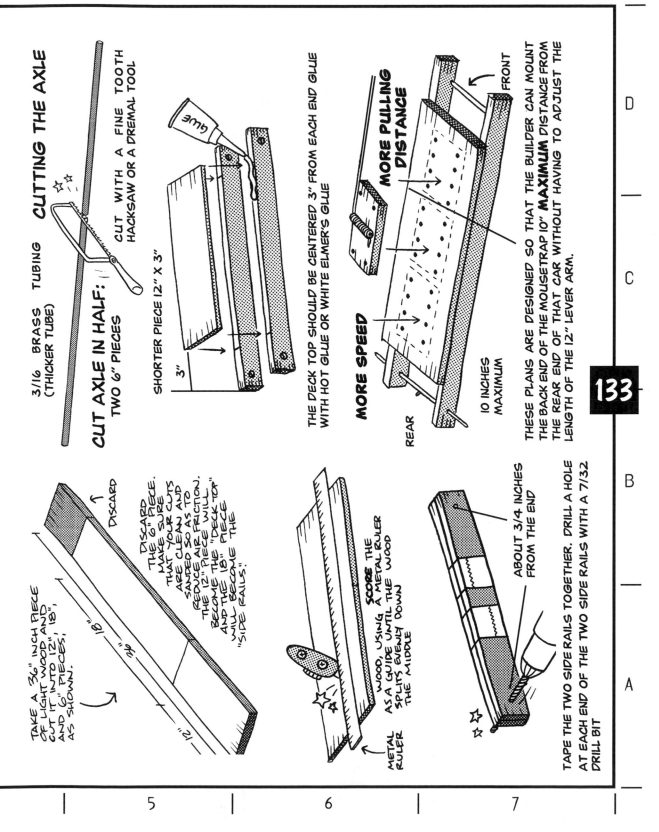

AXLE SET-UP

THE CDS SHOULD BE SUPERGLUED TO THE RUBBER WASHERS AND THEN GLUED TO THE ENDS OF THE AXLE. DO NOT PUSH THEM UP AGAINST THE FRAME. AXLE WITH CDS TURNS FREELY WITHIN THE FRAME. PLACE THE AXLE THROUGH THE HOLES ON EITHER END OF THE FRAME. PLACE A #10 FLAT METAL WASHER ON EACH SIDE OF THE AXLE. PLACE AND MOVE A 1/4-L RUBBER SINK WASHER DOWN EACH SIDE OF THE AXLE UNTIL THERE IS ABOUT 1/8 - 1/4 INCH SPACING BETWEEN THE METAL WASHER AND THE FRAME. *DO NOT GLUE!*

HOOK & LOOP

ON THE FREE END OF THE STRING TIE A LOOP THAT IS LARGE ENOUGH TO CATCH THE HOOK

HOOK AND LOOP ARE DESIGNED TO RELEASE.

LEVER ARM LENGTH

THE LEVER ARM SHOULD BE LONG ENOUGH TO REACH THE DRIVE AXLE AND *NOT* LONGER OR SHORTER. IF YOU TRY MOUNTING THE MOUSETRAP AT DIFFERENT LOCATIONS FROM THE DRIVE AXLE YOU WILL HAVE TO *ADJUST* THE LENGTH OF THE LEVER ARM AND THE STRING BY CUTTING BOTH. IF YOU THINK YOU WILL BE CHANGING THE LOCATION OF THE MOUSETRAP IT IS A GOOD IDEA *NOT* TO GLUE THE TRAP DOWN BUT INSTEAD USE SOME SMALL NUTS AND BOLTS TO HOLD IT DOWN.

MAKING THE AXLE HOOK

TWIST WIRE ON AXLE

TWIST THE SMALL WIRE TIGHTLY AROUND THE DRIVE AXLE (REAR AXLE). *BE CAREFUL!* IF YOU TWIST TOO TIGHT THE WIRE WILL BREAK.

GLUE HOOK TO AXLE

TRIM THE AXLE HOOK WITH A SCISSORS, THE AXLE HOOK SHOULD *NOT* BE LONGER THAN 1/8 INCH.

PUT A COUPLE DROPS OF *SUPERGLUE* ON THE HOOK TO BOND IT WITH THE AXLE.

TIE A LOOP KNOT

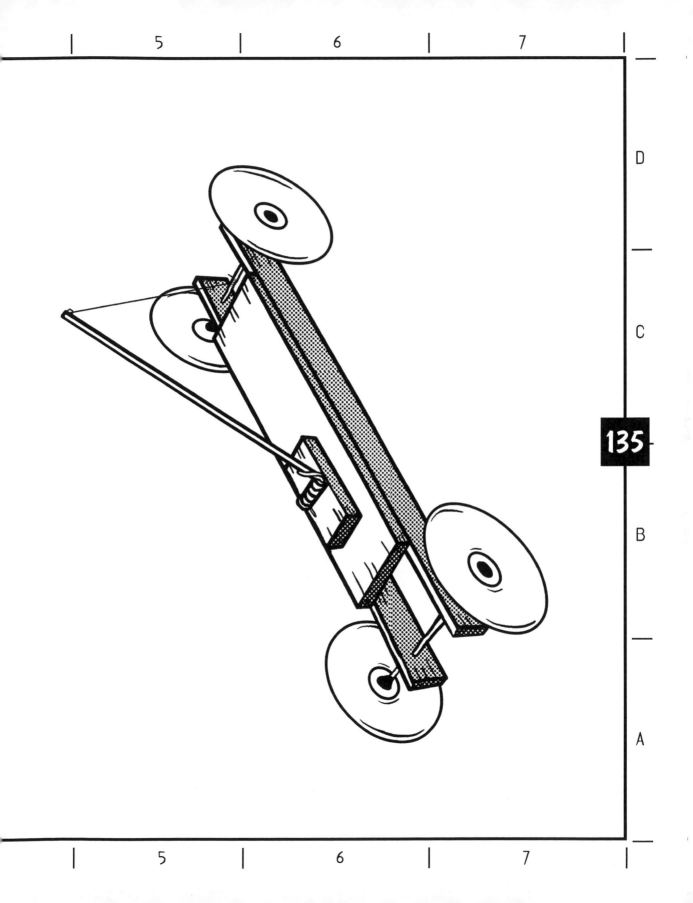

DOC FIZZIX ENGINEERING DEPARTMENT

INSTRUCTIONS FOR MOUSETRAP VEHICLE ASSEMBLY

K-300-DF SPEED-TRAP

PARTS:

1 - VICTOR MOUSETRAP
1 - BASSWOOD STRIP 24X1/4X1/4
1 - BALSAWOOD STRIP 12X1/2X1/4
1 - ALUMINUM TUBE 3/16 X 12
1 - BRASS TUBE 5/32 X 12
1 - BRASS TUBE 1/8 X 12
2 - 2" DIAMETER "LITEFLITE" WHEELS PART# DAV5520
1 - SET OF 5/8" ALUMINUM DRAGSTER FRONT WHEELS
    PART# PARMA 673
1 - 1/16" AXLE FRONT OR BRASS ROD
1 - SET OF 4-40 X 1/2 SOCKET HEAD SCREWS PART #
    GPMQ3012
1 - SET OF 4-40 X 1/2 BLIND NUTS PART # GPMQ3324
1 - PICTURE WIRE (3 INCHES)
1 - KEVLAR FISHING LINE (12 INCHES)
2 - SEA #10 METAL FLAT WASHERS
2 - 1/4 L RUBBER SINK WASHERS
4 - MICRO-BEARINGS (3/16 INNER DIAMETER) - OPTIONAL

DO NOT GLUE!

DO NOT GLUE!

DO NOT GLUE!

1/8 INCH BRASS TUBE
CUT TO 6 INCHES

GLUING THE FRAME TOGETHER

THE SMALL BLOCKS OF WOOD ARE GLUED TO THE REAR END OF THE FRAME. TAKE CARE TO LINE UP THE HOLES IN THE SMALL BLOCKS ACROSS FROM ONE AND ANOTHER AS YOU GLUE THEM TO THE REAR END OF THE FRAME OR THE CAR WILL NOT TRAVEL STRAIGHT. GLUE THE FRAME PIECES TO THE SIDE OF THE MOUSETRAP. THE FRONT EDGE OF THE FRAME SHOULD BE ALIGNED WITH THE FRONT EDGE OF THE MOUSETRAP. THE FRONT EDGE OF THE MOUSETRAP IS THE END THAT THE MOUSETRAP'S SNAPPER ARM IS POINTING.

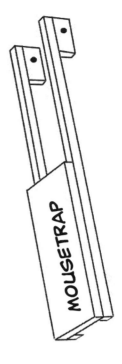

MOUSETRAP

137

CUTTING SIDE RAILS

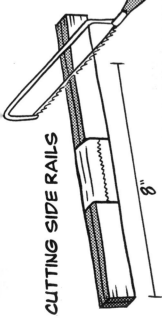

8"

TWO SIDE RAILS ARE CUT TO A LENGTH OF 8 INCHES. THE SIDE RAILS ARE CUT FROM A 1/4 INCH WIDE BY 1/4 INCH THICK BY 16 INCHES OR MORE PIECE OF BASSWOOD.

MAKING THE AXLE SUPPORTS

1 1/2"

TWO AXLE SUPPORTS ARE CUT TO A LENGTH OF 1 1/2 INCHES FROM A PIECE OF BALSA WOOD THAT IS 1/2 INCHES WIDE BY 1/4 INCH THICK AND 3 INCHES IN LENGTH OR MORE.

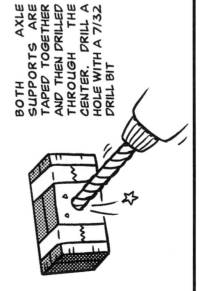

BOTH AXLE SUPPORTS ARE TAPED TOGETHER AND THEN DRILLED THROUGH THE CENTER. DRILL A HOLE WITH A 7/32 DRILL BIT

MAKING THE DRIVE AXLE

CUT WITH A FINE TOOTH HACKSAW OR A DREMAL TOOL

THE AXLE CONSISTS OF TWO PARTS, A 4 3/4 INCH LONG BRASS TUBE CUT FROM A 5/32 TUBE, AND A 3 1/4 INCH BRASS TUBE CUT FROM A 3/16 INCH TUBE. THE 3/16 TUBE WILL BE GLUED WITH SUPER GLUE OVER THE 5/32 INCH TUBE.

3/4"

3/4"

SUPER GLUE TUBES TOGETHER

3/4"

SLIDE REAR WHEELS ONTO REAR AXLE

MAKING THE FRONT AXLE SET-UP

CUT FROM "REQUIRED MATERIALS #3"

3"

1"

CORING SAW

CUT ONLY HALFWAY THROUGH

1" x 1"

BRASS COLLARS NEED TO BE CAREFULLY GLUED IN PLACE. DO NOT GLUE TIGHTLY AGAINST WHEELS

DO NOT GLUE!

DO NOT GLUE!

THE SWIVEL BASE IS ATTACHED TO TO THE BOTTOM OF THE AXLE HOLDER EXTENSION USING A SMALL SCREW AND BLIND NUT. THE AXLE SHOULD BE SANDWICHED BETWEEN THE AXLE HOLDER EXTENSION AND THE SWIVEL BASE. DO NOT OVER TIGHTEN THE SCREW, YOU SHOULD BE ABLE TO TURN THE SWIVEL BASE TO ADJUST THE STEERING. GLUE SET-UP TO THE FRONT OF THE RACER, THE SET-UP MOUNT SHOULD EXTEND ABOUT 1 1/2 INCHS FROM THE FRONT OF THE VEHICLE.

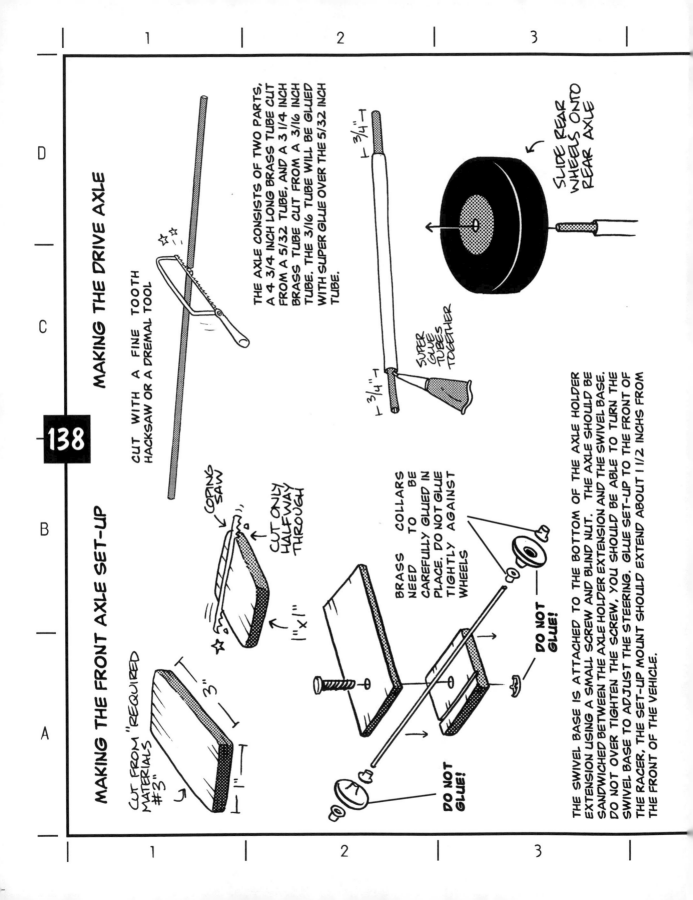

AXLE SET-UP

THE CD'S SHOULD BE SUPERGLUED TO THE RUBBER WASHERS AND THEN GLUED TO THE ENDS OF THE AXLE. DO NOT PUSH THEM UP AGAINST THE FRAME. AXLE WITH CD'S TURNS FREELY WITHIN THE FRAME. PLACE THE AXLE THROUGH THE HOLES ON EITHER END OF THE FRAME. PLACE A #10 FLAT METAL WASHER ON EACH SIDE OF THE AXLE. PLACE AND MOVE A 1/4-L RUBBER SINK WASHER DOWN EACH SIDE OF THE AXLE UNTIL THERE IS ABOUT 1/8 - 1/4 INCH SPACING BETWEEN THE METAL WASHER AND THE FRAME. **DO NOT GLUE!**

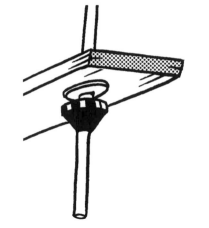

HOOK & LOOP

ON THE FREE END OF THE STRING TIE A LOOP THAT IS LARGE ENOUGH TO CATCH THE HOOK

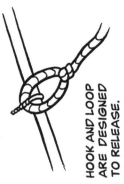

HOOK AND LOOP ARE DESIGNED TO RELEASE.

LEVER ARM LENGTH

THE LEVER ARM SHOULD BE LONG ENOUGH TO REACH THE DRIVE AXLE AND **NOT** LONGER OR SHORTER. IF YOU TRY MOUNTING THE MOUSETRAP AT DIFFERENT LOCATIONS FROM THE DRIVE AXLE YOU WILL HAVE TO **ADJUST** THE LENGTH OF THE LEVER ARM AND THE STRING BY CUTTING BOTH. THE STRING SHOULD "JUST" REACH THE DRIVE AXLE OR BE A LITTLE SHORTER SO THAT IT FULLY RELEASES FROM THE AXLE HOOK AND DOES NOT GET TANGLED OR RE-WIND.

MAKING THE AXLE HOOK

TWIST WIRE ON AXLE

TWIST THE SMALL WIRE TIGHTLY AROUND THE DRIVE AXLE (REAR AXLE). **BE CAREFUL!** IF YOU TWIST TOO TIGHT THE WIRE WILL BREAK.

GLUE HOOK TO AXLE

TRIM THE AXLE HOOK WITH A SCISSORS, THE AXLE HOOK SHOULD **NOT** BE LONGER THAN 1/8 INCH.

PUT A COUPLE DROPS OF **SUPERGLUE** ON THE HOOK TO BOND IT WITH THE AXLE.

TIE A LOOP KNOT

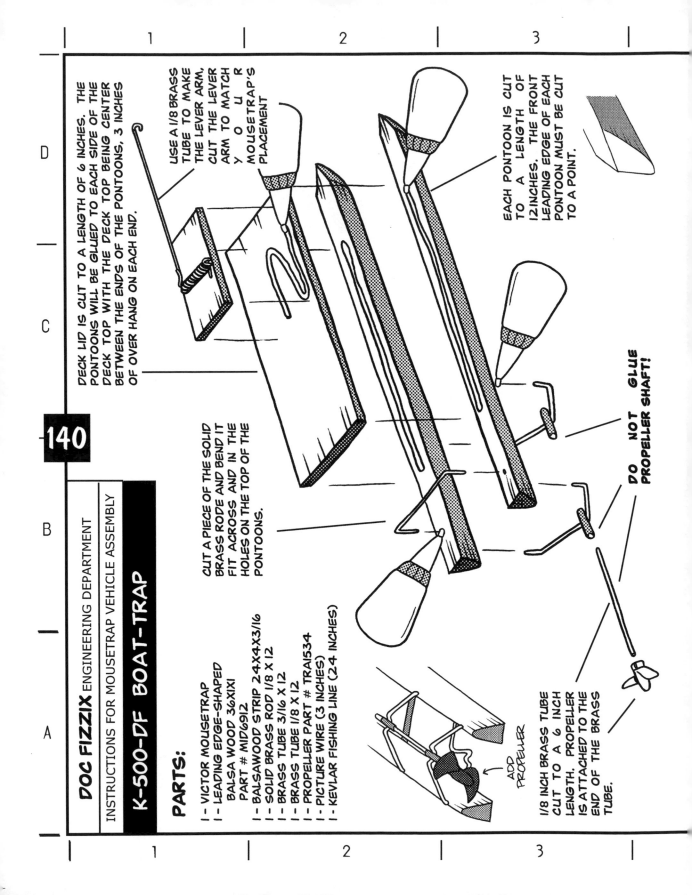

DOC FIZZIX ENGINEERING DEPARTMENT

INSTRUCTIONS FOR MOUSETRAP VEHICLE ASSEMBLY

K-500-DF BOAT-TRAP

140

PARTS:

1 - VICTOR MOUSETRAP
1 - LEADING EDGE-SHAPED BALSA WOOD 36X1X1 PART # MIP6912
1 - BALSAWOOD STRIP 24X4X3/16
1 - SOLID BRASS ROD 1/8 X 12
1 - BRASS TUBE 3/16 X 12
1 - BRASS TUBE 1/8 X 12
1 - PROPELLER PART # TRAI534
1 - PICTURE WIRE (3 INCHES)
1 - KEVLAR FISHING LINE (24 INCHES)

DECK LID IS CUT TO A LENGTH OF 6 INCHES. THE PONTOONS WILL BE GLUED TO EACH SIDE OF THE DECK TOP WITH THE DECK TOP BEING CENTER BETWEEN THE ENDS OF THE PONTOONS, 3 INCHES OF OVER HANG ON EACH END.

USE A 1/8 BRASS TUBE TO MAKE THE LEVER ARM, CUT THE LEVER ARM TO MATCH YOUR MOUSETRAP'S PLACEMENT

EACH PONTOON IS CUT TO A LENGTH OF 12 INCHES. THE FRONT LEADING EDGE OF EACH PONTOON MUST BE CUT TO A POINT.

CUT A PIECE OF THE SOLID BRASS RODE AND BEND IT FIT ACROSS AND IN THE HOLES ON THE TOP OF THE PONTOONS.

DO NOT GLUE PROPELLER SHAFT!

1/8 INCH BRASS TUBE CUT TO A 6 INCH LENGTH. PROPELLER IS ATTACHED TO THE END OF THE BRASS TUBE.

ADD PROPELLER

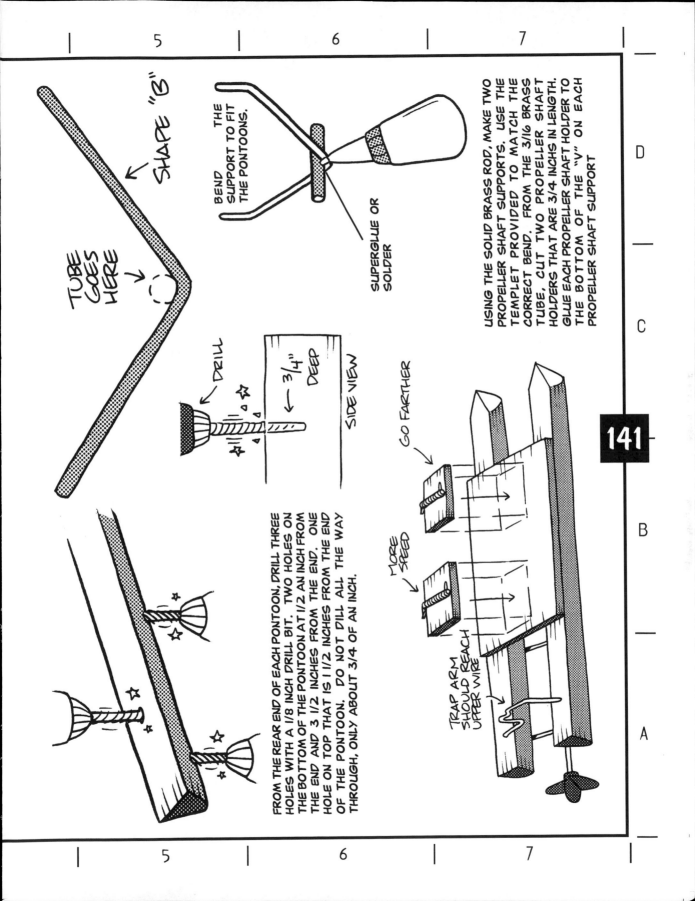

SHAPE "B"

TUBE GOES HERE

THE BEND SUPPORT TO FIT THE PONTOONS.

SUPERGLUE OR SOLDER

USING THE SOLID BRASS ROD, MAKE TWO PROPELLER SHAFT SUPPORTS. USE THE TEMPLET PROVIDED TO MATCH THE CORRECT BEND. FROM THE 3/16 BRASS TUBE, CUT TWO PROPELLER SHAFT HOLDERS THAT ARE 3/4 INCHS IN LENGTH. GLUE EACH PROPELLER SHAFT HOLDER TO THE BOTTOM OF THE "V" ON EACH PROPELLER SHAFT SUPPORT

DRILL

3/4" DEEP

SIDE VIEW

GO FARTHER

MORE SPEED

TRAP ARM SHOULD REACH UPPER WIRE

FROM THE REAR END OF EACH PONTOON, DRILL THREE HOLES WITH A 1/8 INCH DRILL BIT. TWO HOLES ON THE BOTTOM OF THE PONTOON AT 1/2 AN INCH FROM THE END AND 3 1/2 INCHES FROM THE END. ONE HOLE ON TOP THAT IS 1 1/2 INCHES FROM THE END OF THE PONTOON. DO NOT DILL ALL THE WAY THROUGH, ONLY ABOUT 3/4 OF AN INCH.

TIE A LOOP KNOT

GLUE HOOK TO AXLE

TRIM THE AXLE HOOK WITH A SCISSORS, THE AXLE HOOK SHOULD **NOT** BE LONGER THAN 1/8 INCH.

HOOK & LOOP

ON THE FREE END OF THE STRING TIE A LOOP THAT IS LARGE ENOUGH TO CATCH THE HOOK

HOOK AND LOOP ARE DESIGNED TO RELEASE.

THE STRING SHOULD BE "JUST" LONG ENOUGH TO EACH FROM THE TIP OF THE LEVER ARM, OVER THE SOLID BRASS ROD BETWEEN THE TWO PONTOONS, AND DOWN TO THE HOOK ON THE PROPELLER SHAFT. THE LEVER ARM SHOULD BE CUT SO THAT, WHEN THE STRING IS FULLY WOUND AROUND THE PROPELLER SHAFT, THE LEVER ARM IS DIRECTLY ABOUT THE HOOK ON THE PROPELLER.

MAKING THE HOOK

AXLE HOOK SHOULD BE PLACED DIRECTLY UNDER UPPER WIRE PIECE

ROD PUSHED FORWARD

UPPER WIRE PIECE

TWIST WIRE ON AXLE

TWIST THE SMALL WIRE TIGHTLY AROUND THE PROPELLER SHAFT. **BE CAREFUL!** IF YOU TWIST TOO TIGHT THE WIRE WILL BREAK. THE HOOK SHOULD BE POSITIONED DIRECTLY BENEATH THE BRASS RODE GOING ACROSS THE TOP OF THE PONTOONS.

SIDE VIEW

PLACE AXLE HOOK HERE

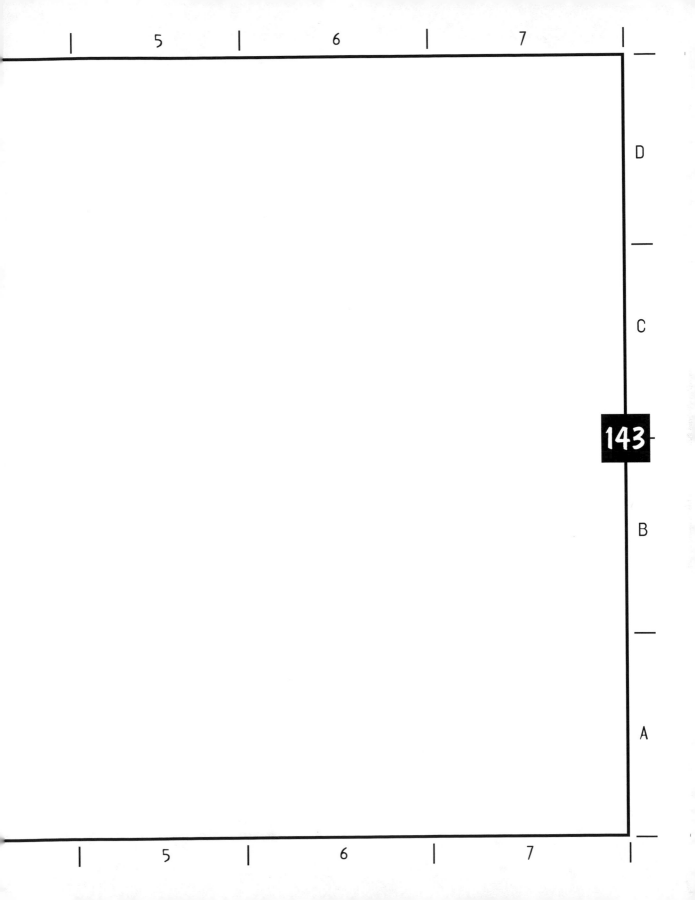

143

OBJECTIVE:

Build a vehicle powered solely by the energy of one standard-sized mouse trap (1 3/4" X 3 7/8") that will travel the greatest linear distance.

By definition, a vehicle is "a device with wheels or runners used to carry something (e.g., car, bus, bicycle or sled)." Therefore, launching a ball (e.g., marble) from the mouse trap will be ruled illegal.

REGULATIONS:

1. The device must be powered by a single "Victor" brand mouse trap (1 3/4" X 3 7/8"). Other brands may be used if permitted.
2. The mouse trap can not be physically altered except for the following: 4 holes can be drilled only to mount the mouse trap to the frame and a mouse-trap's spring can be removed only to adjust the length of its lever arm.
3. The device cannot have any additional potential or kinetic energy at the start other than what can be stored in the mouse-trap's spring itself. (This also means that you cannot push start your vehicle.)
4. The spring from the mouse trap cannot be altered or heat treated.
5. The spring cannot be wound more than its normal travel distance or 180 degrees.
6. Vehicles must be self-starting. Vehicles may not receive a push in the forward direction or side direction.
7. The vehicle must steer itself. Measurements of distance will not measure the total distance traveled, only the displacement distance.
8. Distance will be measured from the front of the tape at the starting line to the point of the vehicle that was closest to the start line at the time of release.
9. The instructor has the final decision as to the appropriateness of any additional items that might be used in the construction of the vehicle.

RUNNING THE CONTEST:

1. The race track can be any smooth level floor, a gymnasium or a non-carpeted hallway.
2. Each contestant will be given three attempts. The winner will be that vehicle which has obtained the greatest distance on any one of the three attempts. Any ties will be decided by a single run-off between the vehicles which tied.

The Great Mouse-Trap Car Speed Race Rules

OBJECTIVE:

Build a vehicle, powered solely by the energy of one standard-sized mouse trap (1 3/4" X 3 7/8") that will travel a 5-meter linear distance in the shortest amount of time.

By definition, a vehicle is "a device with wheels or runners used to carry something (e.g., a car, bus, bicycle, or sled)." Therefore, launching a ball (e.g., a marble) from the mouse trap will be ruled illegal.

REGULATIONS:

1. The device must be powered by a single "Victor" brand mouse trap (1 3/4" X 3 7/8") Other brands may be used if permitted.
2. The mouse trap can not be physically altered except for the following: 4 holes can be drilled only to mount the mouse trap to the frame and a mouse-trap's spring can be removed only to adjust the length of its lever arm.
3. The device cannot have any additional potential or kinetic energy at the start other than what can be stored in the mouse-trap's spring itself. (This also means that you cannot push start your vehicle.)
4. The spring from the mouse trap cannot be altered or heat treated.
5. The spring cannot be wound more than its normal travel distance or 180 degrees.
6. Vehicles must be self-starting. Vehicles may not receive a push in the forward direction or side direction.
7. The vehicle must steer itself. Measurements of distance will not measure the total distance traveled, only the displacement distance.
8. Vehicles can not receive a running start and must start as close as possible to the start line. Time of run will begin when any part of the vehicle passes over the start line and will ends when that same point passes over the 5-meter mark.
9. The instructor has the final decision as to the appropriateness of any additional items that might be used in the construction of the vehicle.

RUNNING THE CONTEST:

1. The race track can be any smooth level floor, a gymnasium or a non-carpeted hallway.
2. Each contestant will be given three attempts. The winner will be that vehicle which has obtained the least amount of time on any one of the three attempts. Any ties will be decided by a single run-off between the vehicle which tied.

The Great Mouse-Trap Car Breaking Rules

OBJECTIVE:

Build a vehicle, powered solely by the energy of one standard-sized mouse trap, (1 3/4" X 3 7/8"), that will travel a 5-meter linear distance in the shortest amount of time AND stop as close to the 5 meter mark as possible without going over.

By definition, a vehicle is a device with wheels or runners used to carry something, as a car, bus, bicycle, or sled. Therefore, launching a ball, such as a marble from the mousetrap will be ruled illegal.

REGULATIONS:

1. The device must be powered by a single Victor brand mouse trap (1 3/4" X 3 7/8") Other brands may be used if permitted.
2. The mousetrap can not be physically altered except for the following: 4 holes can be drilled only to mount the mousetrap to the frame and a mousetrap's spring can be removed only to adjust the length of it's lever arm.
3. The device cannot have any additional potential or kinetic energy at the start other than what can be stored in the mouse trap's spring itself. (This also means that you cannot push start your vehicle.)
4. The spring from the mousetrap cannot be altered or heat treated.
5. The spring cannot be wound more than its normal travel distance or 180 degrees.
6. Vehicles must be self-starting. Racers may not receive a push in the forward direction or side direction.
7. The vehicle must steer itself. Measurements of distance will not measure the total distance traveled only the displacement distance.
8. Racers can not receive a running start and must start as close as possible to the start line. Time of run will begin when any part of the vehicle passes over the start line and will ends when that same point passes over the 5-meter mark.
9. The instructor has the final decision as to the appropriateness of any additional items that might be used in the construction of the vehicle.

RUNNING THE CONTEST:

1. The race track can be any smooth level floor, a gymnasium or a non-carpeted hallway.
2. Each contestant will be given three attempts. The winner will be that racer which has obtained the lowest score on any one of the three attempts. Any ties will be decided by a single run off between the racers that tied.

SCORING: lowest score wins:

Score = (time in seconds) + (distance from 5 meter mark in centimeters) + (distance OVER 5 meter mark in centimeters)
Note: the penalty for going over the mark is the distance from the line being added twice, if a car does not go past the line then the distance over the line is zero.

The Great Mouse-Trap Boat Race Rules

OBJECTIVE:

Build a vehicle, powered solely by the energy of one standard-sized mouse trap (1 3/4" X 3 7/8") that will travel a 3-meter linear distance in the shortest amount of time.

By definition, a vehicle is "a device that floats such as a boat." Therefore, launching a ball (e.g., a marble) from the mouse trap will be ruled illegal.

REGULATIONS:

1. The device must be powered by a single "Victor" brand mouse trap (1 3/4" X 3 7/8") Other brands may be used if permitted.
2. The mouse trap can not be physically altered except for the following: 4 holes can be drilled only to mount the mouse trap to the frame and a mouse-trap's spring can be removed only to adjust the length of its lever arm.
3. The device cannot have any additional potential or kinetic energy at the start other than what can be stored in the mouse-trap's spring itself. (This also means that you cannot push start your vehicle.)
4. The spring from the mouse trap cannot be altered or heat treated.
5. The spring cannot be wound more than its normal travel distance or 180 degrees.
6. Vehicles must be self-starting. Vehicles may not receive a push in the forward direction or side direction.
7. The vehicle must steer itself. Measurements of distance will not measure the total distance traveled, only the displacement distance.
8. Vehicles can not receive a running start and must start as close as possible to the start line. Time of run will begin when any part of the vehicle passes over the start line and will ends when that same point passes over the 3-meter mark.
9. The instructor has the final decision as to the appropriateness of any additional items that might be used in the construction of the vehicle.

147

RUNNING THE CONTEST:

1. The race track can be any body of water that is greater than 3-meters.
2. Each contestant will be given three attempts. The winner will be that vehicle which has obtained the least time on any one of the three attempts. Any ties will be decided by a single run-off between the vehicle which tied.

Mouse-Trap Car Worksheet

 What is the diameter of your vehicles drive wheels?

 What is the circumference of the drive wheels?
The circumference is calculated by multiplying the drive wheel diameter by Pi or 3.14.

 How far will your vehicle travel in one rotation of the drive wheels?
A vehicle will travel the same distance as the circumference for each turn of the drive wheel.

 What is the diameter of the drive axle?

 What is the circumference of the drive axle?
The circumference is calculated by multiplying the drive axle diameter by Pi or 3.14.

148

 How much string is used during one complete turn of the drive wheel?
In one turn of the axle, the length of string used is the same as the circumference.

 What is the length of your vehicles power stroke?

For your vehicles power stroke, how many times would the string wind around the drive axle? (Note, the string should always be as long or a little shorter than the power stroke.)
The number time that the drive axle turns during the power stroke is calculated by dividing the length of the power stroke by the amount of string needed for one turn of the axle.

How many turns will the drive wheel(s) make during the power stroke?
same number as the turns of string around the axle

How far will your vehicle travel during the power stroke?
Multiply the drive wheel circumference by the turns of string.

Mouse-Trap Car Worksheet

☐	Mouse-Trap Car's Mass
☐	Mouse-Trap Car's Weight
☐	Normal Force on non-drive wheel(s)
☐	Normal force on drive wheel(s)
☐	Position of center of mass from non-drive wheel(s)
☐	Rotational inertia of non-drive wheel(s)
☐	Rotational inertia of drive wheel(s)
☐	Wheel grip or traction force
☐	Coefficient of Traction
☐	Coefficient of rolling friction
☐	Friction force of non-drive wheel(s)
☐	Maximum Acceleration
☐	Drive Wheel Axle Radius
☐	Drive Wheel Radius
☐	String Tension at start
☐	Potential energy of wound mouse-trap
☐	Predicted travel distance
☐	Actual travel distance
☐	Speed over 5 meters